WAR IN THE PACIFIC

The most important, explosive, and strategic battles of World War Two took place in the Pacific arena, as the seemingly invincible Japanese sought to expand their notorious empire. Now this astonishing era comes to life in a breathtakingly authentic new series by noted historian Edwin P. Hoyt that places the reader in the heart of the earth-shattering conflict—a dramatic, detailed chronicle of military brilliance and extraordinary human courage on the bloody battlefields of the land and sea.

VOLUME
I

TRIUMPH OF JAPAN

WAR IN THE PACIFIC

VOLUME I

TRIUMPH OF JAPAN

EDWIN P. HOYT

AVON BOOKS ◆ NEW YORK

WAR IN THE PACIFIC, VOLUME I: TRIUMPH OF JAPAN is an original publication of Avon Books. This work has never before appeared in book form.

AVON BOOKS
A division of
The Hearst Corporation
105 Madison Avenue
New York, New York 10016

CONTENTS

1.	Preparations	1
2.	Psychology of War	18
3.	Pearl Harbor	26
4.	Grand Sweep Plan	39
5.	The Tiger in Malaya	46
6.	Invading the Philippines	53
7.	Bataan	68
8.	The Fall of Singapore	84
9.	Striking the Indies	92
10.	The Juggernaut Advances	99
11.	Invading Java	104
12.	The Japanese Move In	113
13.	End of the Asiatic Fleet	125
14.	Conquest of Java	131
15.	The Fall of Bataan	138
16.	Death March	147
17.	Japan's War	156
18.	The Americans Strike Back	165
19.	Trincomalee	170
20.	Air Raid on Tokyo!	175
21.	High Tide	183
	Bibliographical Notes	186
	Index	191

ONE

Preparations

It is hard to believe that a tiny military force of 12,000 men could force a nation of 100,000,000 people into a policy that the public did not want and toward a war that no responsible national leader desired. And yet that is almost precisely what happened in Japan in 1931 when a group of young colonels precipitated the Mukden incident that led to the Japanese occupation of the six northeastern provinces of China and the establishment of the puppet state of Manchukuo—and the Pacific war.

It is true that the atmosphere within the imperial Japanese army lent itself to the purposes of the plotters. It is also true that many general officers were eager to see the army in control of Japanese political life. This in itself was nothing either new or startling; in the 1920s, when this plot was building, the Meiji Constitution was only half a century old, and Japan had a much longer history of government by the military than that. The word *shogun* in Japanese means "general," and shoguns governed Japan from the 13th century until nearly the end of the 19th century. Even under the Meiji emperor's rule many of the cabinet ministers were military men, and only in the later years of the Meiji era did civilian politicians and political parties make their appearance.

1

The military had always found the civilian politicians to be a sharp pain in its collective side, and the reason was simple enough. The military wanted expansion; the civilians wanted to keep taxes down. Japan nearly bankrupted herself fighting the Russo-Japanese War, but the military expected Japan, as the victor, to secure a huge cash payment from Russia as the spoils of war. Japan did not get it because of the civilians and Theodore Roosevelt, who managed the peace treaty and showed mercy to the Russians. The American role in that treaty, incidentally, was one of the underlying causes of the Pacific war; the Treaty of Portsmouth tagged America as the enemy of Japan's military establishment.

The military was built up again to fight in World War I but in 1919 the civilians again cut it back. Then came hard times for Japan and the growing anger of the young officers, many of whom came from peasant families that were literally starving in the 1920s. The answer by the militarists was a drive for colonies and resources. Virtually every young officer was enlisted in that cause. The results were Mukden, Manchukuo, and the push for control of Inner Mongolia and northern China.

After 1932 the pressure in China was constant, with the Japanese establishing and then enlarging a garrison at Tianjin. The fever of Japanese expansionism in China came to a head in the summer of 1937 with a new incident in northern China. The place was the Marco Polo Bridge just outside Beijing. The incident was precipitated by a Japanese training unit, which was passing a Chinese military unit on the bridge. Firing began and quickly spread. The local Japanese commander called for support; the army in Japan quickly moved to help him by sending three divisions of troops to China to augment the already big Tianjin garrison there, which had burgeoned since 1932 as the Japanese extended their influence in Manchuria and the fringe areas of northern China.

What was really happening was that the Japanese army was following a predetermined plan to take control of all of northern China as well as of Manchuria, and the Chinese had experienced one incident after another since 1932. The Japanese army was determined that this 1937 incident would precipitate real action, and it did. After some stalling, the fighting continued and spread. The three Japanese divisions arrived at Taku near Tianjin. By July 30 they had captured Tianjin and began following a vicious policy of rape and riot among the civil population, which was meant by the Japanese commanders to terrorize the Chinese and make them surrender to the Japanese. The Chinese in northern China did not have the guns, tanks, or planes with which to carry on an extensive war with the Japanese army. They fought in the daytime and retreated at night, a pattern established that summer. On August 4 the Chinese evacuated Beijing; the Japanese immediately occupied the city and established a puppet government for all of northern China.

The Japanese army had expected, with so much of China under its control by that time, that Chiang Kai-shek would sue for peace and the Japanese government would grant that peace in exchange for the right to exploit Mongolia—which the Japanese army saw as a second Manchukuo—and Chinese acceptance of the state of Manchukuo. The Japanese advanced to Shanghai, the pearl of the Yangtze River and the richest and most important city in China. The Japanese demanded the right of penetration of the enormous Chinese market in textiles and household goods. The Japanese, of course, did not call all these actions a war. They were merely another series of "incidents" that could be resolved satisfactorily just as soon as the Chinese accepted the inevitable and yielded to the Japanese demands.

But the Chinese Nationalist government saw that what the Japanese were planning was the total colonization of China, no matter what the Japanese chose to call it. So the Chinese were thoroughly aroused. On August 7 at Nanking, the Chinese National Defense Council mapped out a strategy of sorts. The Council declared that the Japanese were in effect engaged in open war with them and that they, the Chinese, would meet it with a "sustained strategy of attrition.'' This meant a policy of fight and retreat, fight and retreat, retreat and fight, but never capitulate.

This policy soon became a matter of deep concern in Japan. General Hajime Sugiyama, the Japanese war minister, like almost all the other generals in Japan, had favored the expansion into China, expecting that it would go much as had their previous forays into Manchuria and Mongolia. None of the Japanese military had expected the weak Chinese Nationalist government to declare war! Taking their clue from the Kwantung army, now run by General Hideki Tojo, the Japanese military had anticipated a quick victory over the Chinese.

Instead they ran into unexpected resistance. As for the Japanese people at home, all they knew was what they were told by the army or by the newspapers, which since the 1920s had been coerced or bribed into doing the army's bidding. The Chinese resistance to Japanese aggression in northern China was depicted in the Japanese press as the stubborn defiance of a brother who would not listen to reason about what was best for him.

The Japanese foreign office, not yet under the control of the military, deplored the army's actions and tried to stop them. In fact, the foreign minister, Koki Hirota, was actually negotiating with the Chinese. And when Emperor Hirohito expressed his personal concern about the activities of the army to General Sugiyama, the war minister treated the matter as one of little importance and said it would be ended in a month.

The emperor was temporarily pacified by this statement and by the appointment of General Iwane Matsui to head the Chinese Expeditionary Force; General Matsui had long been an advocate of Sino-Japanese cooperation, not confrontation. Of course, the army had engineered Matsui's appointment largely to propitiate the emperor, whose anti-war feelings were well known.

General Matsui went to the palace to accept his official appointment, and when he left he was given a ride in the car of Prince Fumimaro Konoye, the prime minister. Konoye had already been personally requested by the emperor to bring the China incident to a quick end. The diplomats set to work and drew up an agreement for a cease-fire and the disbandment of the puppet government of northern China that had been set up by the overeager Japanese generals.

On August 8 it seemed that the cease-fire might work, but on August 9 a Japanese marine lieutenant was killed in an incident at the Shanghai airfield, and the fuse was lit. The Japanese demanded that the Chinese withdraw all their military forces from the Shanghai area. The Chinese refused; after all this was their country, China, not Japan. That night the Chinese National Defense Council ordered three divisions of Chinese troops to attack the Japanese.

The Chinese divisions moved up to Shanghai University, Chi Chi University, and Paoshan bridge. There they engaged the Japanese marines. Diplomatic negotiations broke down, and on August 13 the Japanese cabinet agreed to the army's request to send two more divisions to "protect Japanese interests" in Shanghai. Prime Minister Konoye and War Minister Sugiyama showed Japanese solidarity by together seeing General Matsui off at the station. The general promised that, since the Chinese would not listen to "reason," he would make a swift capture of their capital city, Nanking, and then they would have to come to terms.

A few Japanese military men, such as Colonel Kanji Ishihara, now began to believe that Japan had gone too far. Ishihara had been one of the architects of the Mukden incident; now he wanted Japan to withdraw from central China.

But the majority of the military men felt the other way.

General Matsui's choice of words in stating his aims in China was unfortunate. It gave the division commanders the impression that they were to turn the troops loose on China, and that any sort of punishment would be justified, to teach the Chinese a lesson quickly.

Matsui landed 35,000 fresh troops at the Yangtze estuary, near Shanghai, on August 23, but it was four months before

Shanghai fell and General Matsui could start his advance up the Yangtze.

Matsui did not move fast enough for the eager men of the army high command in Tokyo. They sent another expedition to China, 60,000 more men under General Heisuke Yanagawa. He and his troops arrived at Hangchow Bay on November 5, 1937. Among the troops was the Sixth Division headed by Lieutenant General Hisao Tani. Tani had instructed his officers to be tough with the Chinese. The Sixth Division began the 40-mile march to Nanking. In three days they had moved 25 miles, burning the countryside as they went as a lesson to the Chinese.

Down from northern China came the Sixteenth Division, under General Kesago Nakajima, a sadist and torturer who encouraged his men in every excess. They began their march to Nanking, burning and looting along the way. Alongside them marched the Eleventh Division, whose commander noted: "Every night from my sleeping floor I could see the glare of the villages they were firing. Only cowards are involved in such incidents."

On marched the Japanese and Chiang Kai-shek tried to interpose more troops. But the Chinese were no match for the skilled and well-equipped Japanese, and by December 7, 1937, General Chiang Kai-shek evacuated Nanking and flew to Hankow, 350 miles up the Yangtze. But he did not surrender.

The Japanese army was furious about that refusal to surrender, because it destroyed all the arguments that had been given the emperor and the diplomats about the manner in which China should be treated in order to force it to accept Japanese domination. So the fierce generals Nakajima and Tani continued to move toward the evacuated Nanking, bent on achieving maximum destruction in order to punish Chiang Kai-shek.

General Matsui, the friend of China, lay bedridden at his headquarters in Suchow, a victim of a tubercular fever. He was, in effect, kicked upstairs, made commander of all Japanese forces in China, and his job as head of the expeditionary force was given to Prince Asaka, uncle of the emperor. Thus the imperial household came to bear the stigma of "personal" responsibility for the events that followed. The Japanese troops, acting under instructions from Imperial army headquarters in Tokyo to "teach the Chinese a lesson," behaved in a completely brutal manner, totally heedless of world reaction. Their purpose was to terrify the Chinese and thus force Chiang Kai-shek's government to come to terms.

Thus came the "rape of Nanking." Japanese troops of two divisions, one led by the notorious General Nakajima, entered the capital city of Nanking. They sealed off the city and for six weeks conducted a campaign of terror, murder, rape, and plunder. Two hundred thousand Chinese died in the destruction, virtually everything that could be carried away was looted, and twenty thousand women were raped, most of them repeatedly night after night.

There had been enough such incidents following the capture of Tianjin and Shanghai to give the Japanese army a bad reputation, but after Nanking, the world pictured the Japanese soldier as nothing more than a ruthless animal. That image was to be reinforced for the next eight years, fueled by reports of the innumerable episodes of terror planned by Japanese army authorities and also by area commanders. For the area commanders had great power over the territories in which they operated, at least until such time as another authority might be established. This policy of terror and rapine was deliberate, a part of the Japanese plan to become masters of Asia and the western Pacific region.

The "other authority" was established in China in March 1940, with the inauguration of the new "Nationalist" government of Wang Ching-wei in Nanking. Wang was an old associate of Chiang Kai-shek and had been the most trusted political assistant of Dr. Sun Yat-sen.

The Chinese retreated first to Hankow and later to Chungking. After the fall of Nanking and the *Panay* incident, in which an American gunboat was sunk, the Japanese asked the Americans to remove their gunboats from the Yangtze River in central China, so there would be no more incidents of that sort. That request was, of course, a warning that the Japanese had no intention of giving up their conquest of China.

The request was made of American Admiral Henry Yarnell, the commander of the U.S. Asiatic Fleet; he politely told the Japanese to go to hell. When Hankow was the capital of China, American and British gunboats were stationed there. But the Japanese marched on, and only too soon Hankow had to be abandoned by the Nationalists. They kept moving west, stopping finally in Chungking, along the farther reaches of the Yangtze in Szechuan province. The U.S. gunboat *Tutuila* was sent there to represent American might, but most of the activity moved to Shanghai.

After the capture of Shanghai it was clear the Japanese had taken over. They requested that all foreign warships visiting Shanghai harbor be cleared by the Japanese shore command before they moved out. Admiral Yarnell again told the Japanese to go to hell. If there had then been more Americans who shared Admiral Yarnell's thinking, the Japanese takeover in Asia might still have been stopped, but there were, unfortunately, too many who were like Admiral William A. Glassford, commander of the Yangtze River patrol, who held the view that since the Japanese now controlled Shanghai, they had to be respected. He did not help matters with that attitude, as the British in Shanghai often told him. But the Glassford view triumphed, and when Admiral Yarnell's tour of duty ended in 1939 and he indicated he would be glad to take another, the navy said no. The navy was prompted by Secretary of State Cordell Hull, who shared Glassford's views and believed that Yarnell had too peppery a personality and might get the United States into trouble. Trouble? What sort of trouble could there have been in standing up to the Japanese? Yarnell knew very well that the only possible way of avoiding war was to confront the Japanese and face them down. To follow the

Glassford-Hull course, he said, would eventually lead to disaster.

The next American commander to take over the Asiatic Fleet was Admiral Thomas Hart. He agreed with Admiral Yarnell that the only way to deal with the Japanese was to be very tough in the face of their demands, but the State Department agreed with Admiral Glassford that temporization was the answer, and so the Japanese continued to have their own way in China. In 1940 President Roosevelt's attention was focused on Europe, where Adolf Hitler's Nazi juggernaut was running amok, and so the State Department view in Asia prevailed and governed policy.

By the fall of 1940, Admiral Hart recognized the weakness of the American position in China, and he moved the command post of the U.S. Asiatic Fleet to Manila. Obviously, the navy said, the United States had no hope of maintaining its presence in China if the Japanese were to extend their activities beyond China's borders, but the Americans could probably hold on to the Philippines, even with the tiny Asiatic Fleet, so small that its flagship was the cruiser *Houston,* not a battleship, as a proper flagship should be, because the fleet did not have a battleship. But Wang's rivalry with Chiang Kai-shek for leadership of the Nationalist movement was intense, and so he allowed himself to be persuaded by the Japanese that theirs was the way of the future, to establish a government subservient to Japan in Japanese-occupied China.

By the end of 1938 the Japanese army had pushed forward to the inland areas of China, and Chiang Kai-shek had established his capital *pro tem* in Chungking. The Japanese strategy took two approaches: military conquest and political persuasion. The latter failed because the Japanese program of horror had antagonized the Chinese people far beyond the limits of President Wang Ching-wei's ability to persuade his countrymen to cooperate with invaders. The military program failed because Chiang continued to exist, to resist, and because, though the Chinese retreated, they never gave up.

The Japanese Imperial Army expanded into Sujou, Guang dong, Wuhan and soon occupied northern and central China. In Japan, the army continued to gain power, until by 1938 it was the most important element in Japanese society, but there were two divisive factions within it. Both factions favored expansion, but one favored expansion north and west by attacking the Soviet Union, while the other wanted to strike south and secure several sources of supply of military resources.

The strike-north faction had its innings first. In 1937, hard on the heels of the launching of the China incident that was supposed to last only 30 days, the ebullient Kwantung army, flushed with its successes in Manchuria and Mongolia, launched a tentative attack against the USSR on the Amur River, using as an excuse a Soviet patrol's movement to the south side of the river, a disputed border point. The Soviet response was immediate and strong. The Japanese lost 25,000 men and retreated.

Another incident occurred in July 1938 at a place called Chankufeng Hill, on the Korean-Siberian border. Here a clash with the Russians cost the Japanese the decimation of a regiment, with 500 troops killed and 900 wounded. The Japanese backed off, badly bruised.

Still, they did not give up their probe north. They launched yet another movement when border units of the Republic of Outer Mongolia and the Manchukuo empire clashed. Since the Outer Mongolians were under the protection of the USSR and the Manchukuo government was a Japanese puppet, the two bigger nations themselves soon became involved. The head of the Kwantung army, without consulting Tokyo, sent a division to the area known as Nomonhon, on the Khalka River. The Soviets also sent troops. Soon the clash became serious, the war ministry in Tokyo was involved, and a real war began, involving tanks, planes, and infantry. So the Kwantung army, on its own initiative, had expanded the war in ferocity, much to the unhappiness of Emperor Hirohito, who, through the war minister, issued a cease-and-desist order.

The fighting continued, however, because the Russians had been truly provoked, and they sent Marshal Zhukov, one of their best generals, to Nomonhon. The Russians mounted an offensive and virtually destroyed the Japanese Twenty-third Division. The Kwantung army, its pride hurt, wanted to put another three divisions into the struggle, but imperial headquarters threatened to cut off the supply of army replacements. The Kwantung army was virtually independent of Tokyo by this time, but it did need Japanese soldiers. So the Kwantung army, its pride and its forces badly beaten, retreated, having suffered some 20,000 casualties. The Japanese army had learned a valuable early lesson: not to bother the Russian bear. So the attention of the army authorities in Tokyo was, in late 1939 and early 1940, focused on the southern regions of Asia.

The Japanese government was put in a virtual state of siege by the army, and by 1939 the army was triumphant. Virtually no civilian politicians were able to form a government. If the army did not like the prime minister designate, it refused to supply a war minister for the cabinet. The law said the army had to provide an active-duty officer for this job, and if the army did not, a cabinet could not be formed.

One of the few politicians acceptable to the army was Prince Konoye, who had been prime minister until January 1939, when he resigned because the army would not end the China incident. Konoye was persuaded to come back into the prime ministry in July 1940. By that time several important changes in the international scene had combined to affect Japan.

First, the Japanese army, after three years of warlike activity in China, was more deeply involved than ever in that country. Each year thousands of new troops were needed to carry on the offensives that had enabled the Japanese to win all the battles and seize all the Chinese towns, but they were unable to quell the people. Also, by treaty, Japan had become a member of the Rome-Berlin-Tokyo Axis, and here its two European partners were winning their battles. France fell to the Germans, and that left the colony of Indochina ripe for Japanese occupation. The Japanese realized Indochina would make an excellent base for a further movement south, into Malay's rich tin-mining country, rubber plantations, and the Dutch East Indies oil fields.

Obtaining oil was, of course, a major problem for Japan. She had almost no oil of her own—only one tiny field up in Niigata prefecture on the northern part of Honshu island. But Java, Sumatra, and Borneo were brimming with oil. The lure was enormous because the Japanese naval, army, and civil planners had realized their current reserves were only barely enough to meet their needs for a little over a year. The primary source of their oil was the United States-and British-controlled companies in the Middle East.

In the fall and winter of 1940–41 anyone who visited Shanghai could feel the tension and the sense of war approaching. The cotton mills of Shanghai were working at about a third of capacity, which infuriated the Japanese who controlled them and made them all the more determined to bring the Chinese Nationalists to their knees and restore the Japanese markets. But the Japanese got nowhere. The Chinese boycotted their products, and this made matters worse, and made Japanese determination turn to fury.

In Shanghai, too, the Japanese tipped their hand, and showed the fate they intended for the whites in Asia. White foreigners were insulted and often physically abused, as was the American consul, John M. Allison, when he was slow to answer a Japanese officer's impertinent questions and was slapped in the face. The Japanese marched along the sidewalks forcing foreigners into the street. Their arrogance toward Westerners was overwhelming, but they were particularly abusive to the Chinese because of the unforgivable behavior of Chiang Kai-shak's continued resistance.

Early in 1941 Admiral Hart saw war coming and began to make what preparations he could in the Philippines. Given the materials with which he had to work, there was not a great deal he could do. A cruiser and a light cruiser or two; a handful of destroyers, mostly overaged; an old aircraft carrier, the *Langley,* so old that she was now capable only of ferrying aircraft, not of launching them; and a fleet of submarines, many of them as superannuated as the destroyers—this was Admiral Hart's fleet.

The admiral rebuilt the mine field that protected Manila Bay and stepped up operations at the Cavite Navy Yard.

President Roosevelt apparently decided that the war clouds hovering over the Pacific and Asia were too gray for his liking. He did not want to be forced into precipitate action in the Pacific when his real interest lay in assisting the British in their hour of need in Europe. So on November 7, 1941, the president ordered all American gunboats withdrawn from China and also ordered the marines out. The only marines who were to stay were those guarding actual diplomatic installations. Admiral Hart then informed Admiral Glassford to begin an orderly withdrawal, and the Americans started evacuating.

The gunboat *Wake* came downriver from Hankow; much to the annoyance of the American sailors, the Japanese insisted on sending warships along to escort them. In Shanghai the *Wake* tied up alongside the other American gunboats *Luzon* and *Oahu.*

On November 29 Admiral Glassford made a sad trip to the offices of the Shanghai Municipal Council, which represented all the foreign settlements, to announce that the Americans were pulling out of Shanghai. He left and got into his car; as he did so, the Japanese commanding admiral came along. Even Glassford was no longer interested in putting on a show of respect, and he sat in his car quite rudely and talked to the Japanese admiral through the car window. The atmosphere between them was hostile. Both knew that war between their nations was just days away. The signs were unmistakable.

Admiral Glassford went back to his shore headquarters and sent a telegram to Admiral Hart, saying that he was leaving China and would try to run down through the Pescadores with the little gunboat fleet, expecting to arrive in Manila about December 4. But he did not know if the uncertain peace would last that long. Every sign pointed to a Japanese move in the very near future, and Admiral Glassford told Admiral Hart that if necessary he would make for Hong Kong and shelter there.

In the months after the Japanese "rape of Nanking" and their concomitant attack on several foreign gunboats in the Yangtze River and the sinking of the U.S. gunboat *Panay*, American sympathy toward China and enmity toward Japan increased enormously. These sentiments led to an increase in American aid to China over the Burma Road from Rangoon across the Himalayas. The Japanese tried to interdict the traffic with air raids but were not notably successful. What they needed to control southeast Asian traffic were airfields farther south. The opportunity to gain them came with the fall of France and her occupation by the Nazi allies of Japan.

On September 22, 1940, the Japanese marched into French Indochina, declaring that the French had invited them in to help put an end to the "China incident" and restore peace and order to Asia. In Japan this action was explained as necessary because "the outlaw Chiang Kai-shek" had created a new war zone in southern China. Chiang was now called an outlaw because the Japanese had recognized as legitimate their puppet government headed by Wang Ching-wei, which they had set up.

The British had closed down the Burma Road during the Japanese air raids, but when the Japanese moved their operations to Indo China, the British opened the road once again.

The United States delivered a grim warning to the Japanese: President Roosevelt cut off all shipments of iron and steel and scrap metal to Japan, which had been America's biggest buyer. Certainly the Americans saw that their iron and steel were being used to make weapons, and in 1940 many of them sensed that the weapons might be turned against them.

So the result of the new Japanese move was to turn the Western powers away from any conciliatory policy toward

Japan. And this attitude was very much resented by the Japanese army.

When Prime Minister Konoye came into office a second time, he accepted the army's choice of General Hideki Tojo as war minister. Tojo had risen swiftly in the ranks of the Japanese army after the Manchurian incident that led to the establishment of Manchukuo. He had then been chief of the *kempei tai*, the military police. Soon he became commander of the Kwantung army and later led a punitive expedition into Mongolia, a foray characterized by forced marches through sleet, snow, and marshes, which showed the strength and resiliency of the Japanese soldier.

Later, in the middle 1930s, Tojo was made deputy war minister, a post he held until he showed his essential arrogance by lecturing a number of industrialists about their responsibility to follow the army way and threatened them if they did not cooperate. Some of those he threatened were members of the largest Zaibatsu firms, and they complained of his highhandedness to the cabinet. Tojo was hastily relegated to a new post as inspector of military aviation.

He had now come back to assume full stature as war minister, in which post he had the complete support of his fellow generals. In the preceding two years war minister had become the most important post in the cabinet. The prime minister existed only by the grace of the army, which could pull him down at any time simply by refusing to let a general serve as war minister. So the cabinet now was pledged to fulfill the army aims.

The signing of the tripartite pact that formed the Rome-Berlin-Tokyo Axis came five days after the march into Indochina, and the combination of events made the world shudder. *Mainichi Shimbun,* one of Japan's most important newspapers, gave the popular view: "The time has at last arrived when Nippon's aspiration and efforts to establish East Asia for Asiatics, free from the Anglo-Saxon yoke, coincides exactly with the German-Italian aspiration to build a new order in Europe and to seek a future appropriate to their strength by liberating themselves from the Anglo-Saxon clutches . . .''

New Order in Asia. The term was coined by Prince Konoye. What it meant was the emergence of the Asiatics from beneath the colonial wing. Because no matter what else would be said about Japanese ambitions and actions, it would have to be recognized that they were prompted partially by a deep Japanese sense of inferiority to white people, an attitude that struck a sympathetic chord throughout Asia.

This sort of thinking had become popular in Japan during the euphoria that followed in the wake of its successes in the China adventure. (In fact, the establishment of the New Order was the most lasting change to come from the entire Japanese military adventure of the 1930s and 1940s. Japan's actions precipitated the revolution of the colonial peoples of Asia, and although Japan lost the Pacific war, Asia would never again be the same; five years after the end of that war all the countries of Asia would be either free or struggling for freedom.)

It is certain the Japanese recognized the importance of the moment. Historians delved into the hazy, mythological early history of Japan and emerged with the conclusion that the year 1940 was the 2600th anniversary of the founding of the nation. So an enormous celebration was held. Hirohito and his empress came out of their usual seclusion to hold a reception in the outer garden of the palace for 50,000 notable citizens. A military musician wrote the ''26th Century March,'' and the military bands played it with great enthusiasm. Hirohito issued an official announcement, the significance of which was lost on most of his listeners:

''It is our earnest hope that peace will be restored soon and that we may share with all countries happiness and prosperity, albeit the world is now in the midst of great turmoil. . . .''

The day was January 1, 1941.

In a surge of enthusiasm, the political leaders of Japan vowed to give up their rights, abandon their political parties altogether as the army wanted them to do, and join the cause of the *Gumbatsu*, the military hierarchy that by 1938 had taken control of the destiny of Japan.

Assessing the situation a quarter of a century after the war, the editors of *Mainichi* blamed the politicians, the press, and, by implication, Emperor Hirohito, for the drift toward war:

"On January 1, 1941, Japan was being prepared for war. That, however, did not necessarily mean that the war was absolutely unavoidable. Had the nation's politicians been more firmly resolved to fulfil their political duties, had the journalists been determined to supply the nation with such information as might prove painful for their readers to swallow, Japan would not have taken the deadly course that it eventually did. The fact is that those who could have acted otherwise stayed inactive and irresponsible as they watched the hope for peace slip out of Japan's hand."

There *was* hope for peace—but not among the army generals. The military faction had the bit in its teeth and was bent on conquest. The only way to avoid war was for those who stood in Japan's way to submit, and the Chinese, British, Americans, and Dutch, who were obviously such obstacles, were not prepared to do that. So by the summer of 1941, the active-duty army was ready, even if the national leaders claimed they were serious in their search for peace. Almost everything happening in Japan pointed toward war.

TWO

Psychology of War

In 1940 and early 1941 the Japanese were a sorely beset people. The army knew, after more than three years of fighting in China, that the Japanese military was sinking into a morass. But there was no way out without losing face. The American "demand" that the Japanese withdraw from China only made it more certain that the Japanese would refuse to accede.

And everywhere, in every department, the Japanese prepared for war.

The navy's Admiral Isoroku Yamamoto, commander of the Combined Fleet, devised the basic Japanese attack plan for the Pacific war. Yamamoto personally did not want war with the United States and Britain; he was certain that it would end in disaster for Japan. But in 1940, when it became apparent that the army was indeed pulling Japan into war, Yamamoto planned an attack that was designed to immobilize the American fleet for at least a year. Yamamoto would follow the pattern cut by Admiral Heihachiro Togo in the battle against the Russian Far Eastern Fleet at Port Arthur a half century earlier. The Yamamoto plan called for the use of half a dozen carriers acting in concert—the first time carriers had been so employed in the modern world. When the plan was revealed, it occasioned considerable adverse comment in the navy department, for this sort of employment of carriers was totally revolutionary and very dangerous. If things went wrong, Japan could lose most of her carrier force in one battle, said the traditionalists. True, said Yamamoto, but it was better to die all at once rather than by inches. If Japan tried conventional warfare against the United States she would most certainly lose.

The battleship admirals were very uneasy about the Yamamoto plan. He had always been something of a "Peck's bad boy" of the navy; he had been slated to be a gunnery expert and had changed over to the air service, learning to fly after he was forty years old.

The argument simmered in the halls of the navy ministry for weeks. Finally, however, Admiral Yamamoto had his way, because he persisted in the argument that only by defeating the Americans at the outset did Japan have a chance of winning the war. So most of the year 1941 was devoted by the navy to planning the preemptive strike and training for it at sea, largely at Kagoshima, on the southern tip of Kyushu, where a mock-up of the Pearl Harbor facilities was built for practice purposes. Specially designed aerial torpedoes, set to explode properly in shallow water, were devised by the experts for the attack fleet.

Day after day for months the pilots came screeching across the mountains and down the gorge to practice dropping torpedoes on the mock-up that was so much like Pearl Harbor. At sea the captains of war ships were assigned to night exercises without lights, keeping formation in all sorts of weather. It was the sort of discipline designed to turn a navigator's hair gray. At nearby airfields the pilots of the level bombers practiced formation flying and tight bombing. The pilots of fighters and dive bombers practiced alone as well until their proficiency was such that they were taken out on their carriers for proving operations.

Only a handful of the leaders knew what they were practicing for, but all of them knew it meant war, and they were eager for the fray.

Army training took on a different tone, after War Minister

Hideki Tojo produced a pamphlet called *Senjinkun,* a new code for the Japanese soldier. This document had been prepared under Tojo's guidance and was presented for imperial approval early in January 1941. It was approved, although the emperor was not very happy with the implication in the pamphlet that those who died had died for him. In the years since 1935, the army had developed a new Bushido, based loosely on the old samurai warrior code of honor above life but embroidered with the new army's trappings.

The new army held that the emperor was divine, a being above men, and that the lives of every person in the Japanese empire had to be dedicated to the imperial service. There was no greater honor for a soldier than to die fighting for the emperor, said the pamphlet, and so echoed the officers who interpreted it to the men.

"Do not dishonor your names," said *Senjinkun.* "Strong are those who know shame. You must always be aware of the honor of your kinsfolk, and strive not to betray their expectations. Don't stay alive in dishonor. Don't die in such a way as to leave a bad name behind you."

By the spring of 1941, many military leaders of Japan had some private questions about what was going on, particularly in China. That huge land mass was eating up soldiers, equipment, and money. The Japanese won nearly every battle, but the vanquished Chinese would disappear, regroup, and come back to fight again somewhere else. Japanese victory became meaningless. Casualties were high, and the Chinese fought well if they were well led, well equipped, and well fed. Some of them were. But as time went on, it became apparent to the Japanese that the Nationalist forces were not pressing the war. The Chinese Communists in the north were fighting very hard with primitive equipment and harrying the Japanese garrisons constantly. But in south and central China, Chiang Kai-shek seemed more concerned with what the Communists were doing than with what the Japanese were up to. Several efforts were made by Japanese leaders to try to end the

China incident, but Chiang Kai-shek would not join forces with Wang Ching-wei as the Japanese insisted.

By the summer of 1941, Prime Minister Konoye was thoroughly disillusioned. War seemed inevitable. He had asked for a summit conference with President Roosevelt and had been turned down on procedural grounds; there was no point in holding a summit meeting, the Americans felt, until the basic points involved had been agreed upon by the two governments.

The Americans held that the basic issue was the continued presence of the Japanese army in China. And the Japanese held that the presence of that army was nothing more than an "incident" and that the soldiers were really protecting Japanese business interests, as well as defending the Chinese people against that bandit Chiang Kai-shek. Prince Konoye, who had been expecting some sort of magical solution if he could but sit down with President Roosevelt, was greatly disappointed. By midsummer he scarcely knew where to turn.

During this critical period imperial conferences were held frequently, sometimes more than twice a week. With each conference the drift toward war became more pronounced.

On September 5, Emperor Hirohito summoned General Sugiyama, the army chief of staff, to his presence. What had happened to that promise, now so long ago, that the China incident would be ended inside of six months? The air between emperor and general was heavy. And so too was the air around navy chief of staff Osami Nagano, who had also been summoned.

The emperor wanted to know just how prepared the army and navy were to carry on military operations. Sugiyama answered that the army was ready to capture Malaya and the Philippines in less than five months. The emperor did not believe the general. He thought Sugiyama was boasting and he said so. He reminded Sugiyama once more of the promise Sugiyama had made as war minister: to bring a quick end to the China incident. And now the emperor asked Sugiyama if he was really sure he could win the war.

Sugiyama was certain and said so. He was much embarrassed by the imperial questioning, because it indicated both disapproval and distrust on the part of his sovereign. For his part, Emperor Hirohito did not like anything he was hearing. He said to the general and the admiral:

"Do your best to solve problems peacefully through diplomacy. This should not go parallel with military preparations for war but should be given priority."

Sugiyama's heart dropped. He believed not in negotiation but in the power of the sword.

The next day the Supreme War Council met with the emperor, who sat at the head of the table, saying very little.

"Holding with the wish to maintain its self-defense and self-preservation, the Empire, resolved to dare a war with the U.S. and Britain and Holland, will attempt to complete its military preparations by the end of October," said the generals and admirals. This point of view was enthusiastically endorsed by Yosuke Matsuoka, one of the major Japanese supernationalists since the days when he helped plot the takeover of Manchuria as president of the South Manchurian Railroad. Matsuoka was foreign minister in the Konoye cabinet. "The Empire will concurrently further its efforts to fulfill its objectives through negotiation with the U.S. and Britain," said the conferees. Everyone knew that this was scarcely more than giving lip service to the emperor's wishes. The fact was that the Supreme War Council was already moving toward war:

"The Empire, with determination to deploy its military forces in the beginning of December, will make its efforts to complete operations plans. Diplomatic conference with the U.S. will be continued."

Of course it was continued, and it would be strengthened with the addition of another envoy, but no one really had any faith in the idea of diplomacy except the emperor. And since the others had no faith, they made no move in that direction.

By the first of October, Prime Minister Konoye had completely lost faith in his ability to avoid war, so he resigned.

Now, since there was no civil leader to whom the army was willing to give power, General Tojo succeeded to the prime ministry, and thereafter the course of Japan was resolutely set toward war.

Hirohito made another attempt to stop the drift toward war. On the October day that General Tojo was slated to become prime minister, he went to the palace to receive the order to form a cabinet. The emperor ordered Tojo to retract the decision of September 6 to follow a dual policy of negotiation and armament. The emperor said he wanted the new cabinet to start with a blank sheet of paper.

General Tojo dutifully so told his new cabinet, but his words carried no conviction.

To justify their thinking, the new leaders of Japan invented a new concept. As the leaders of America, China, Great Britain, and the Netherlands observed the Japanese move into Indochina and their ongoing penetration of China, they formed a joint defense policy to counter a Japanese attack. The Japanese complained that this policy was encirclement by ABCD—America, Britain, China, Dutch—and that the purpose of the defense alliance was to put Japan down.

On December 1, 1941, the Supreme War Council referred to the "failure of diplomatic negotiations," and said that the empire would enter a state of war with the U.S., Britain, and the Netherlands.

And so diplomacy and the emperor's efforts to force the generals to use it instead of military weapons came to the end of the line.

Admiral Glassford did not know it when he set sail from Shanghai that late November day in 1941, but the Japanese fleet was already at sea, the striking force heading for Pearl Harbor and the other elements of the fleet going about their appointed tasks that would lead the Japanese navy and army to Malaya, the Philippines, and the Pacific islands.

In Washington, the navy knew that something was up, for American agents in various parts of the Pacific had sighted elements of the Japanese fleet. Admiral Harold Stark, chief of naval operations, issued a war warning to the Asiatic and Pacific fleets in November. Thereafter, the admiral said, the fleets were to be ready for anything, particularly a Japanese attack.

". . . the number and equipment of Japanese troops and the organization of naval task forces indicates an amphibious expedition against either the Philippines, Thailand, or the Kra peninsula or possibly Borneo . . . ."

Yes, the Allied agents had seen something, but it wasn't the Japanese striking force that was heading swiftly and silently across the northern Pacific toward Hawaii.

So Admiral Glassford sailed from Shanghai in his flagship, the gunboat *Luzon,* and took along the *Oahu.* He had just seen the last of the Fourth Marine Regiment off on the USS *President Harrison.* As the gunboats pulled out, they left behind a seaman, a cook, and four mess attendants who did not make ship in time. After a few days of "freedom" from military discipline, they would be among the first hostages of the Japanese.

The gunboats headed for the Saddle islands, beyond the Yangtze River estuary. They were river gunboats, not meant for work at sea, and this would be a desperate voyage for them if the weather acted up.

The weather was fine as the gunboats headed out. They passed a Japanese warship whose captain was more than a little curious and brought his ship to within five hundred yards of them but finally turned away. The gunboats changed course in the morning and soon met the minesweeper *Finch* and the salvage ship *Pigeon,* which would accompany them to Manila. On December 1 the American ships were approaching the Pescadores, west of Formosa. There, in Japanese waters, they sighted destroyers and were followed by them for all the rest of the day until past midnight.

On December 2 the weather turned foul, but at least the Japanese ships were gone—they had turned back when the American ships moved out of their territory. The gunboats pitched and tossed all day and night, and at times Admiral

Glassford wondered whether the little flotilla would ever see the Philippines.

Then came the dawn of December 3, with clear skies and quiet seas. The ships soon moved down the west coast of the island of Luzon. And when the crews looked up in the sunshine they saw a flight of B–17 bombers overhead. The planes came down to check the little group of ships, recognized them, and flew low over them in salute and welcome. A little later the submarine *S–36* passed close by and the radiomen exchanged gossip. The little gunboats had come safely to their destination.

THREE

Pearl Harbor

The purpose of the Japanese plan to attack Pearl Harbor was to gain time for Japan to carry out her master plan: "to drive Britain and America from Greater East Asia, and to hasten the settlement of the China Incident." There it was in outline. The Pearl Harbor plan was in a sense diversionary, for the major emphasis was to capture lands and resources in the Pacific, additions that would make the Japanese empire completely self-supporting.

But the Pearl Harbor attack was also symbolic at the same time, and here the quotes are those of Admiral Isoroku Yamamoto, architect of the Pearl Harbor attack plan: "The goal of our nation—all eight corners of the world under one roof—will be demonstrated to the world."

But to Admiral Yamamoto's eye, the Pearl Harbor plan was essential to buy Japan the time to swallow the empire she was now about to attack, and particularly to turn the Dutch East Indies into part of the Japanese war machine.

The objections of the conservative elements in the Japanese navy to this plan were overcome by January 1941, even though, during war games, the attacking Japanese force "lost" two of its six carriers. Of course, there was a chance they might lose carriers, said Yamamoto; one did not win victories without taking chances. But the prize was the U.S.

Pacific Fleet and domination of the Pacific for a time—however long it would take the Americans to recover—and the prize was worth the risk, Yamamoto insisted.

By September all the plans were complete. The decision was to make the Pearl Harbor raid simultaneous with the general move south into Malaya, the Philippines, and the smaller islands of the Pacific. Some staff officers wanted to follow the Pearl Harbor attack with an amphibious landing and capture the Hawaiian Islands, but Yamamoto had no interest in this project. Strike, destroy, and get out—that was his plan. It was his firm belief that only by dealing the Americans a heavy blow at the outset of the war would Japan have any chance of achieving her aim of empire.

"I can run wild for a year or even eighteen months," Admiral Yamamoto told the critics of his plan, "but after that . . ."

The Pearl Harbor plan was devised to give the Japanese a quick victory in the hope that the Americans could then be persuaded to come to the peace table and allow Japan to reap the fruits of battle in the southern seas.

Navy Chief of Staff Admiral Osami Nagano agreed with Admiral Yamamoto. In a meeting of the cabinet, when the prospects of war were under discussion, he made a very frank speech.

"As for war with the United States," said Nagano, "although there is now a chance of achieving victory, the chances will diminish as time goes on. By the later half of next year, it will already be difficult for us to cope with the United States; after that the situation will become increasingly worse. The United States will prolong the matter [of peace discussions] until her defenses are built up and then try to settle. Accordingly, as time goes by, the Empire will be put at a disadvantage. If we could settle things without war, there would be nothing better. But if we conclude that conflict cannot be avoided, then I would like you to understand that as time goes by we will be in a disadvantageous position. Moreover, if we occupy the Philippines it will be easier, from the navy's point of view, to carry on the war."

Thus were the Philippines finally included in the plan for attack in the South Pacific, included because of the wishes of the navy.

Actually, the navy did not really care much about the Philippines. Admiral Nagano was representing the position of Yamamoto and others who did not want the war, and he was trying to show the immense difficulties it would bring. Occupation of the Philippines would entail the use of several divisions of troops. Nagano was trying to bluff the army into backing off from the war issue altogether.

But the army would not back off. Occupation of the Philippines was perfectly all right with them. There were plenty of divisions, now and in the offing. Manpower was not a basic problem. The whole nation was on a war footing already, and millions of young men were being siphoned into the service.

General Tojo was now leading the cabinet toward war and everyone could see it.

On September 3 the Japanese leaders held a seven-hour conference that dealt with all the aspects of the war and concluded that the armed forces had no alternative but to forge ahead and maintain the initiative in deciding when they would begin hostilities.

The army was in a particularly belligerent mood and wanted to strike south first; then, having assured the flow of oil and rubber, the Japanese would prepare to strike at the Soviet Union, as Japan's ally Hitler wanted them to do.

As for the attack on the United States, it was now accepted doctrine.

By the first of September almost all the major problems had been discussed and decided, including the route—to the north, for a surprise attack, although the weather forecast was bad.

The six aircraft carriers that were to be used in the raid were assembled, and 423 aircraft were placed aboard them: high-level bombers, dive bombers, torpedo bombers, and fighter planes.

On October 5, 1941, Admiral Yamamoto assembled the

squadron leaders of the air groups aboard the carrier *Akagi* and told them the plan, under strictures of secrecy. The senior officers of the task force were also informed.

Even as these preparations went forward, Nagano, navy chief of staff, continued to worry about the wisdom and chances of success of the Pearl Harbor plan.

The naval general staff finally gave official approval to the Pearl Harbor operation, and Admiral Yamamoto issued his operation orders. December 8 was set for Y-Day, attack day, because it was a Sunday and the Japanese naval staff knew (from espionage intelligence) that it was the habit of Admiral Husband E. Kimmel, chief of the U.S. Pacific Fleet, to bring the fleet into Pearl Harbor for the weekend so that the men could have time for rest and recreation. To the Japanese this custom was an indication of softness of the Americans; their own men had been training for weeks and months with virtually no leave. The Japanese naval leaders tended to sneer at the Westerners and predicted a swift Japanese victory in the war to come.

Next the leader of the attack was chosen: Vice Admiral Chuichi Nagumo. Nagumo was not Admiral Yamamoto's choice—far from it. They were men of widely divergent views; for one thing, Nagumo belonged to the "fleet" faction of the navy, which had long pushed for the use of heavy armament and possible war. Admiral Yamamoto, on the other hand, was a staunch advocate of the "treaty" faction of the navy, which held that it would be suicidal for Japan to attack the United States or Britain and that the terms of the naval disarmament plans of the 1920s and 1930s, limiting the Japanese navy to two-thirds the size of the British and American fleets, were to be borne without rancor.

But there was far more to their differences than that: style, for one thing. Yamamoto was a gambler and a hard leader. Nagumo was much softer and had none of the derring-do about him. He was extremely conservative in his views of action possibilities, and he did not understand the functions and capabilities of carriers very well. He was like the "battleship admirals" of the American fleet, who felt that a carrier was too important and delicate to risk in a major fight.

The fact is that Yamamoto had very little use for Vice Admiral Nagumo and would never have chosen him to lead the attack. But Yamamoto did not have the privilege of making that choice: that authority was jealously held by the naval general staff in Tokyo, and they chose Admiral Nagumo, almost completely on the basis of seniority.

On November 10, 1941, the strike force sailed out from the naval base at Kure, not all the ships at once but in groups. They headed for Hitokappu Wan on the island of Etorrofu, the largest of the Kuriles, north of Japan proper and a desolate fishing ground. The island consisted of snowbound land, a wireless station, a pier, and three fishermen's huts.

Before the fighting fleet sailed, scores of ships had carried oil and provisions to the little island and put them ashore. Now the supplies were brought aboard the warships. It was cold, wet, hard work, but it was completed by December 2, and the fleet sailed from the bay bound for war.

There was still a slight chance that the fleet might not attack. Two Japanese ambassadors were just then in Washington conferring with Secretary of State Hull and other American leaders, trying to work out the differences between the two countries. But the same problem still existed: the Americans insisted the Japanese evacuate China, and the Japanese were determined to continue their struggle to bring the Chinese into the Greater East Asia Coprosperity Sphere, which was their dream of an Asian federation led by, and dependent on, Japan.

If the differences could be worked out, and until the last Admiral Yamamoto hoped against hope they could be, the fleet would be called back.

"Called back?" demanded some of the officers when Yamamoto told them of the possibility. Called back? How could a war fleet be called back once it had been set in motion?

"Called back!" said Admiral Yamamoto grimly. And if any of the officers did not believe in obeying orders, it was time for them to resign their commissions.

So the objections were stilled, but the feeling of nearly all the men of the fleet was expressed by one seaman as he faced the prospect of an attack on Hawaii.

"What will the people at home think when they hear the news? Won't they be excited? I can see them clapping their hands and shouting with joy."

And, although the people at home did not even suspect what was about to happen, they were ready for war, primed by four long years of constant propaganda favoring the China war and the expansion of Japan. Steadily in the past four years the feeling of Japanese toward outsiders had grown ever more inimical. The people had been brainwashed into believing it was Japan's destiny to lead Asia against the white men.

And so the Japanese raiding fleet steamed on across the Pacific.

Admiral Yamamoto's order came on November 25:

"Advance into Hawaiian waters and upon the very opening of hostilities attack the main force of the United States Fleet in Hawaii."

But Yamamoto's caveat remained, indicating his personal hopes. Also, Yamamoto had ordered the fleet to maintain a close radio watch. If the fleet was discovered—which they would learn by monitoring messages from Pearl Harbor—the Japanese were to abandon the mission and return to Japan.

"Should the negotiations with the United States prove successful, the task force shall hold itself in readiness forthwith to return or reassemble."

At six o'clock on the morning of November 26, 1941, the Japanese fleet sailed through a storm and in thick fog; six aircraft carriers in two parallel columns with a battleship bringing up the rear of each column and accompanied by cruisers, destroyers, and submarines.

The weather was stormy all the way, which was the reason

the raiding fleet proceeded undetected. On December 1 the Japanese cabinet ratified the decision by General Tojo to start the war on December 8. Next day Admiral Yamamoto sent the fateful message:

"Niitaka Yama Nobore"—Climb Mount Niitaka—which was the final order to attack on December 8.

And the fleet steamed on, tension growing by the hour.

On December 6 Admiral Nagumo received what his air operations officers considered to be disappointing news: word had come from their spies in Hawaii that seven U.S. battleships, seven U.S. cruisers, and a number of other ships of the American fleet were anchored at Pearl Harbor, but no carriers were present.

On the night of December 7 (December 6, Hawaii time) the seamen aboard the Japanese carriers were summoned to the flight deck of each. The battle flag that had flown over Admiral Togo's ship at the battle of Tsushima was flown from the masthead of the *Akagi*. It was a reminder of a great day, the day that the Japanese had decisively defeated the Russians in the Russo-Japanese war. The ships' captains and the air group commanders made highly emotional speeches, calling on the fliers to do their best and smash the enemy.

At six o'clock in the morning the cruisers launched float planes, which flew over the Hawaiian Islands and ascertained that the American fleet was really there.

Just after the search planes were sent out, the strike force was assembled on the decks of the carriers and began to take off. The weather was very rough. The spindrift scoured the decks of the pitching carriers as the pilots boarded their planes. And then, one by one, the planes took off, 40 torpedo planes, each carrying one of the special torpedoes made just for this attack, weapons that had all the power of the Japanese "long lance" torpedoes but were set to operate in very shallow water, which was what they would find at Ford Island anchorage, where the American fleet lay.

Then 49 more high-level bombers and 51 dive bombers,

escorted by 43 Zero fighter planes, took off. The planes climbed to almost 10,000 feet.

For the Americans, the first sign that something might be wrong was detected by Ensign R. C. McCloy of the USS *Condor*, a small minesweeper that was making a sweep of the harbor entrance. All was quite routine—but at 3:42 in the morning, Ensign McCloy sighted the periscope of a midget submarine just two miles outside the harbor entrance buoy. The *Condor* passed the word by blinker light that it had seen a periscope, and the destroyer *Ward* came in for a look.

At 5:42 a PBY flying boat spotted either that midget submarine or another (several were operating in the area) and dropped smoke pots at the location. The *Ward* came up, spotted the midget submarine, attacked, and sank it with gunfire and depth charges.

At 6:54 A.M., the *Ward* sent a message in code to the commandant of the American Fourteenth Naval District. But the message was delayed because the yeoman who took it, not realizing its importance, gave it no special attention. As a result, the duty officer did not get the message for eighteen minutes. Two more destroyers were then ordered into action. The duty officer tried to call Admiral Kimmel, commander of the Pacific Fleet, but the switchboard was busy with calls being placed by officers arranging golf games and other diversions with their friends for that morning, and the officer had trouble getting through. So it was 7:25 before Admiral Kimmel got the message. As soon as he did he set out for his office.

But foul-ups by navy personnel continued. They were still operating in the relaxed, routine mode of a peacetime navy.

The destroyed midget submarine, launched by a bigger submarine standing off shore, had followed an American warship through the antisubmarine net before it was attacked by the *Ward*. Two other midget subs had also gotten through the net, which had been left open because someone forgot to close it! So Pearl Harbor, the home of the American fleet, was left unprotected from submarine attack for nearly four hours!

Just before 7:40 local time, the Japanese fliers sighted the Hawaiian coastline. Ahead and below they saw the Waianae and Koolau mountains; south of them, sparkling in the sunshine, lay Pearl Harbor and its great fleet.

Pearl Harbor was still asleep in the morning mist, calm and serene, without even a trace of smoke from the stacks of any ship in the harbor. There was no movement on shore; the sailors were still asleep in their barracks on that lovely Sunday morning. Ahead was Ford Island, with its battleships anchored companionably two by two.

At 7:30 A.M. the first Japanese planes reached the attack zone, but they followed instructions and waited for the other planes to arrive so they could make a concerted attack. On the ground, some alert seamen saw them circling but thought they were American planes from American carriers.

At 7:55 the fireworks began. The Japanese planes had all arrived and they plunged in to attack, the level bombers from high altitude, the dive bombers screeching down, and the torpedo bombers coming in low toward Ford Island and dropping their torpedoes. Three minutes later the harbor was ablaze, ships were sinking, and men were dying and struggling to escape the steel coffins that were taking them down to a watery grave.

By 8:25 four separate torpedo-bomber attacks had been made. Immediately after the torpedo planes attacked, the dive bombers, level bombers, and fighters also attacked. Half an hour after the battle began, the battleship *Arizona* was wrecked and burning; the *Oklahoma* had capsized; the *West Virginia* had sunk; the *California* was sinking; and the *Maryland*, *Tennessee*, and *Virginia* were all damaged, as was the repair ship *Vestal*.

Only the battleship *Pennsylvania*, which was in drydock, remained undamaged. The old battleship *Utah*, which had been converted into a target ship for gunnery, took two torpedoes and sank. The light cruiser *Raleigh* was bombed.

Inside the harbor the Japanese midget submarines did their best. One fired a torpedo at the destroyer *Monaghan*. The torpedo missed and exploded against a dock at Pearl City, the *Monaghan* rammed the midget submarine, and that was the end of the two-man crew.

The cruiser *Helena* was torpedoed in the early minutes of the attack by a plane that came in alone. The minelayer *Oglala* was hurt by the same torpedo explosion and capsized. Two destroyers, *Cassin* and *Downes,* were sunk. The destroyer *Shaw* lost her bow. The light cruiser *Honolulu* and the cruiser *New Orleans* were both damaged. A Japanese midget submarine tried to torpedo the cruiser *St. Louis* and failed, and the cruiser sank the midget.

The Americans were fortunate in one thing. So eager were the Japanese fliers to sink battleships that they ignored the tanker *Neosho*, which was loaded with high-octane aviation fuel. If they had set her afire she might have burned down the whole harbor.

The Japanese planes also attacked the naval air stations in the area and destroyed most of the planes. American antiaircraft fire also destroyed some American planes that did get into the air. In all, 2,400 American military men were killed and nearly 1,200 wounded that day. The Japanese losses were very light—29 aircraft and their crews and five two-man submarines.

After the war, historian Samuel Eliot Morison wrote:

"The surprise attack on Pearl Harbor, far from being a necessity as the Japanese claimed even after the war, was a strategic imbecility. One can search military history in vain for an operation more fatal to the aggressor. On the tactical level the Pearl Harbor attack was wrongly concentrated on ships rather than permanent installations and oil tanks. On the strategic level it was idiotic. On the high political level it was disastrous."

But was it?

The fact was that Admiral Yamamoto had counted on finding and sinking the American aircraft carriers. But on the day of the attack the three carrier task forces were all at sea, and the Japanese were unable to locate them.

Admiral Yamamoto had also expected Admiral Nagumo to do a thorough job, which would have meant at least one more day of attack against the Pearl Harbor installations. But Admiral Nagumo was very nervous about the attack in the first place and much afraid of losing carriers. When he could not find the American carriers, he became even more nervous, and the same day as the first attack he pulled away from Pearl Harbor, leaving the job unfinished. Later, when Admiral Chester Nimitz took over the command of the Pacific Fleet, he wondered at the logic of the Japanese, who had left the submarine base and the repair facilities at Pearl Harbor untouched.

The more important error was the failure of the Japanese to cripple the Pearl Harbor submarine base, which they could easily have done with another attack. The spectacular success of the ship attacks seemed to have concealed from Admiral Nagumo the neat rows of fleet-class submarines tied up at their moorings at the base. Also, four-and-a-half million barrels of oil had been stockpiled at Pearl Harbor and most of it, located in dumps above ground, made an easy target. The Japanese ignored them.

So, because of tactical failure, the strategic victory was lost. Another factor that was to mar the victory was totally unperceived even by Admiral Yamamoto, who thought he knew his Americans, having spent several years in the United States early in his career. This was the psychological effect of the Pearl Harbor attack on the United States. Admiral Yamamoto had expected it to leave the Americans stunned and confused. Stunned, perhaps, for a moment. Confused, no. The reaction was fury and a determination to defeat an enemy who had so cowardly attacked before declaring war. Contrary to what Admiral Yamamoto had been told and expected, that is exactly what happened.

Yamamoto had been advised that the Japanese envoys in Washington would break off their talks and issue a declaration of war before his task force struck. It did not happen that way because the Japanese timing was too close. A delay in the communication and translation of the Japanese message to their diplomats in Washington to that effect meant that it arrived after the Pearl Harbor attack, and this infuriated the Americans. The song "Remember Pearl Harbor" was instantly popular in America, and other war morale songs such as "Praise the Lord and Pass the Ammunition" soon followed. The Americans were truly aroused, so aroused that they vowed to fight the Japanese until the enemy surrendered unconditionally.

Admiral Yamamoto, when he learned of what Admiral Nagumo had done, realized, and said so privately, that the Pearl Harbor attack was not the great victory the naval general staff claimed but a failure, because the job hadn't been done right. Of course, Admiral Yamamoto never acknowledged this publicly. For in Japan the attack was greeted with enormous enthusiasm and acclaim, and not even Yamamoto could have made himself heard had he openly objected. On December 8, 1941, all Japan was agog with the news of the major success in the war that had just begun. All Japan was eager to press forward to the victory that would drive the hated white man out of Asia.

As Admiral Nagumo headed nervously for Japan, his ships' radios were tuned in to Radio Tokyo, and they caught the flavor of the excitement that had seized Japan. The announcers needed do little more than read the newspaper headlines that first day; they screamed of the attack on Hawaii; the assaults on Malaya, the Philippines, and Guam; the attack on Hong Kong. Everywhere the Japanese were moving quickly, and the elation of the people at home was enormous.

The emperor commemorated the day with a special Imperial Rescript, officially declaring war on the United States and Britain. The announcement was, of course, overdue; the war had already been going for a day. The rescript spelled out the reasons for war: to save Asia for the Asiatics and to prevent the United States and Britain from disturbing the peace of Asia.

In this heady atmosphere, only Admiral Yamamoto was downcast. He knew that the Nagumo mission had failed in its goal of immobilizing the American fleet and that he would soon feel the unfortunate consequences of his country's actions.

FOUR

Grand Sweep Plan

The way the Pacific War really began has not been well understood in the West, particularly in the United States, where the Pearl Harbor attack on December 7, 1941, is considered to be the major Japanese effort.

But from the Japanese point of view, the attack did not occur on December 7 but on December 8, and it was only part of a major offensive against Malaya, the Philippines, and other areas.

The purpose of the Hawaiian attack was to cripple the American fleet for at least a year, so the Japanese army could pursue its real ambitions, which were to seize needed resources in Southeast Asia to support the war effort to conquer China.

Singapore was attacked from the air. So was Hong Kong. Wake Island was hit, as was Guam, and the invasion forces were off and running. British troops in Thailand were attacked by the Japanese, who crossed the frontier at Battambang and then swarmed across the countryside. They entered Bangkok, the capital, and soon forced the Thai government to sign a treaty with Japan that made Thailand a member of the Greater East Asia Coprosperity Sphere and a Japanese ally in the war. British troops in Thailand, caught by surprise, were quickly overcome. The Japanese military landing force scheduled to attack Malaya made its first landings. On December 8 in Tianjin, a major business city not far from Beijing, the Japanese moved into the international compound. They simply took control and disarmed the foreign soldiers—Americans and British, for the most part. They also took over posts at Tangku, Taku, and Chinwangtao that had been held by foreign troops since the days of the Boxer Rebellion.

It was the same at Shanghai. The Japanese already controlled Shanghai, and had since 1937, but they had left the international settlement alone, and the foreign gunboats that sailed the Yangtze had also been considered sacrosanct. But no longer. In the small hours of December 8, Japanese ships entered the harbor and attacked the foreign gunboats. The British ship *Petrel* fought and was sunk. The captain of the American ship *Wake* was ashore when the Japanese swarmed aboard, terrorized the unwitting crew, and took over the gunboat without a fight.

Ashore, the Japanese troops moved through the international quarter and added that last section of Shanghai to their conquests. It was no longer an international city but a Japanese city on a Chinese shore.

On December 8 the Japanese navy's Vice Admiral Mineichi Koga was given the task of bottling up Hong Kong, and he did so that very day. He blockaded the island with his naval force, while Japanese planes from south China bases bombed the city repeatedly. Within a couple of hours they had wiped out the Hong Kong air force: three torpedo bombers and two amphibious aircraft. While the planes were in the air, troops of the Japanese army's Thirty-eighth Division crossed the frontier. These soldiers had been stationed in Canton for some time, just waiting for this day. They crossed the Sham Chun River and began fighting the British troops, moving toward the New Territories and Kowloon. While Admiral Nagumo, waiting off Pearl Harbor, who had been debating the wisdom of making further attacks and finally decided against the idea, headed back toward Japan, the other army and naval forces involved in this first effort of the war continued to move against their targets.

The major effort on the Asian continent was against Singapore and Malaya, in order to take control of the major British naval base in the East and to guarantee the supplies of tin and rubber the Japanese war machine needed so desperately. How desperately? The Japanese Department of National Planning had reported in July that the stockpile of light oil, used for lubricating the machinery of war, was enough to last only ten days. More had to be imported almost daily to keep Japanese industry and the war machine going. She had only enough kerosene for a month, enough crude oil, used for heating and operating machinery and ships, for only 45 days. A break in the supply of any one of these elements could seriously hamper the Japanese war effort. She also had only enough gasoline for vehicles for about 6 months, and enough aviation fuel, on which the supply men had been concentrating, for 18 months.

The oil the Japanese needed was in the Dutch East Indies, but before they could move there they had first to consolidate their hold on the Southeast Asian continent. That was the reason the Japanese army planners had been working for months to achieve a swift victory in Malaya.

In the spring of 1941 a number of Japanese army officers, thinly disguised as traveling salesmen, went out to Malaya, Hong Kong, the Philippines, and Indonesia to investigate suitable landing sites for amphibious invasions. The officer who headed the Malaya force was a Major Nakasone. He and his other "salesmen" could be seen at strange tasks, measuring the depth of the water along the beaches, checking their tides and the angle of their slopes, and generally examining the terrain—without revealing, of course, their interest in its strength and ability to handle tanks.

They came back to report that the best place to land was at the Isthmus of Kra, a narrow neck of land that joins Thailand and Malaya. This observation was the result of three months of intensive study, during which they pinpointed three small fishing ports: Singora and Pattani in

Thailand, fifty miles from the Malay border; and Khota Bharu, a northern port on the east coast of Malaya at the mouth of the Kelantan River, ten miles south of the Thai border. Each town had a good airfield nearby.

Major Nakasone told the Imperial General Staff that he favored the Singora landing above the others because Singora had a flat beach with rice fields, not cliffs, behind it. What could be more suitable?

Pattani, Nakasone said, was almost as good. He did not like Khota Bharu because of the muddy rivers around it.

Imperial Headquarters decided to make Singora the main landing site but also to land troops at the other two sites to confuse the British.

Down from his post in Manchuria, to which he had been exiled by his old enemy, General Tojo, came Lieutenant General Tomoyuki Yamashita, one of Japan's most brilliant generals, to command this very important invasion of Britain's Malayan colony. As he prepared to assume command of the invasion, his troops were training in amphibious warfare. The training took place in a secluded area of the Inland Sea near Hiroshima. The troops were the Fifth Division and the Eighteenth Division.

Soon the troops were moved down to Hainan Island and alerted to be ready for action at any time. A third division of Imperial Guards was also ready, and a fourth, the Fifty-sixth Division, was held in reserve.

General Yamashita learned only on the eve of assuming command that he would command these divisions. But they had been cut and streamlined, so that instead of the usual division of 36,000 men, each of these was down to 12,000. Yamashita would thus start his amphibious invasion with 24,000 men, who would be joined by the Imperial Guards, which would add another 12,000 men; he would have only 12,000 more men available in case of emergency. This number was in sharp contrast with the British forces in Malaya, then estimated by the Japanese high command to be at least 100,000 men.

In the second week of November, General Yamashita

flew first to Taiwan and then to Saigon, where he called on Field Marshal Count Terauchi, who had secured his transfer from Manchuria so he could take on this important command. For the next few days it was one conference after another—with the Southern Region Headquarters staff; with the navy, which would escort the amphibious landing force; and with Prince Takeda, a member of the Imperial family, who would carry the news of the coming landings to Emperor Hirohito.

After a week in Saigon, Yamashita flew to Hainan to look over the main element of his fighting force. He found the troops already boarding the craft that would take them to the mainland. Yamashita boarded his headquarters ship, the *Ryujo Maru*. Then he waited because it had been impressed on him that the entire situation might change if the negotiations with the Americans were successful. But on November 30 Yamashita had a message from Tokyo:

"X-Day December 8. Proceed with plan."

So the invasion of Malaya and the Philippines was scheduled to coincide with the Pearl Harbor attack and the assault on a number of Pacific islands.

For weeks General Yamashita had been planning, and now he pulled forth his pocket diary and marked the date, January 26, 1942—the date on which he intended to begin the assault on Singapore, the great fortress of Asia.

Another major Japanese target was the Philippines. This one gave the planners a good deal of trouble. The naval staff would have liked to have coordinated the attack on Manila and Manila Bay with the Pearl Harbor attack, but that was impossible because of the time difference between Pearl Harbor and Manila. When it was early morning in Hawaii, it was still dark in Manila. So the Japanese knew that by the time they could attack successfully in the Philippines, the Americans would have been forewarned by what had happened in Hawaii.

The Japanese had other problems. They had never developed a long-range bomber, and the medium bombers stationed on Taiwan did not have the range to strike the airfields of the Clark Field complex near Manila. Since Admiral Yamamoto had preempted six carriers for the Pearl Harbor operation, there was only one carrier, the 10,000 ton *Ryujo,* to operate in the Philippines. This created much concern among the naval general staff, particularly since the Americans had some 50 B–17 long-range bombers stationed at Clark Field.

From the American point of view the Philippine Islands presented a major defense problem, for their combined coastlines were greater than that of the United States, and the total strength of the American and Filipino defense forces in the Philippines at the end of November 1941 was 31,000 officers and men, plus ten reserve divisions about which no one knew much and in which no one had much faith.

The Japanese claimed that the Americans, British, Dutch, and Chinese had planned to encircle them. But the fact was that except for a meeting or two of high-level officials to consider a plan for mutual defense, nothing had been done about it by the end of November 1941.

The British certainly suspected what was coming by September, when the Konoye cabinet collapsed and General Tojo took the helm of state in Japan. But the British in 1941 were besieged in Europe and they had precious little aid available to send. For example, in Malaya, the defense plan called for 48 infantry battalions and two armored brigades. But actually only 33 battalions were available in November, and most of those were Indian troops who had been given very little training.

The Malayan defense was supposed to have a modern air force, but in fact the air force consisted of 141 planes, most of them obsolete.

The only possible hope for shoring up the defenses lay with the Royal Navy. Winston Churchill decided to send the battle cruiser *Repulse* and the new battleship *Prince of Wales* to Singapore, to be joined there by the carrier *Indomitable*. The *Repulse* and the *Prince of Wales* arrived at Singapore on December 4, but no carrier; the *Indomitable* had run aground in the West Indies, and there was no carrier to replace her. So the British force that came to deter the Japanese was, in effect, no deterrent at all.

But General MacArthur thought the American Asiatic Fleet and the American and Filipino land forces could deny the Japanese a victory in the Philippines, while Winston Churchill believed the ships he had sent to the East could protect Singapore.

The one Allied leader who saw clearly what was about to happen was South African Field Marshal Jan Smuts, hero of the First World War, who looked east and told Churchill that if the Japanese with their powerful fleet had their wits about them, they were capable of creating a first-class disaster for the American and British navies.

Deep in the Pacific lie a number of strategically important islands. The Japanese war plan called for the Gilbert Islands, Guam, and Wake to be taken in the initial operations. Next they would move into the Bismarck Archipelago and then on to Papua New Guinea, with an eye to attacking Australia.

And so, as the Japanese Pearl Harbor attack force left its home waters, many other units of both sides also moved down the line, readying themselves for those critical first two weeks of December 1941, which would change the history of the world and the faces of Asia and the Pacific.

FIVE

The Tiger in Malaya

On the eve his troops sailed from Samah, Hainan's port, General Yamashita discovered that the Japanese army did not have a single detailed map of Singapore, the objective of his campaign. Nor were there good maps of any part of Malaya. Yamashita found himself forced to rely on maps from school atlases. The airfields were not shown, and the only way he had of knowing about them was through the work of those "traveling salesmen" who had marked down the locations of the airfields on their hand-drawn maps.

The British had a pretty good idea of what the Japanese were going to do. As a staff officer in Malaya, General Arthur Percival had already considered what form an attack would take and had accurately assessed it. He thought the Japanese would attack Singora, Pattani, and Khota Baru, and that was precisely where they were going.

In the months when Major Nakasone and his fellow officers were spying out the facts of Malaya, so also were British officers dressed in civilian clothes spying on the activities of the Japanese; they achieved a pretty accurate assessment of what targets the Japanese were considering and what tactics they were planning.

By the autumn of 1941 the British were expecting an attack on Malaya, at the places mentioned earlier, and expecting it to come before December 10. They had developed a defense plan—Plan Matador—which would mean sending troops to the Singora and Pattani beaches, but since the plan called for moving troops across independent Thailand's territory, the British war office decided it would not be employed unless specifically sanctioned by the cabinet. That meant the British were ready to meet the invaders on the beaches, in theory but not in fact.

Early on the morning of December 4 the Japanese invasion force sailed from Hainan, bound for the three landing areas; 11 troopships headed for Singora, 6 ships for Pattani, and 3 for Kota Bharu. The force was protected by 2 cruisers and 10 destroyers, along with 5 submarines, but only the submarines went out with the ships when they sailed. The main force was two hundred miles at sea and would meet the convoy only when it neared the coast of Thailand.

Two days later the convoy met its battle force off Point Camau, the southern tip of Indochina.

The convoy steamed on. On December 6, the Japanese sighted two Hudson reconnaissance planes and immediately took evasive action. The ships sailed into the Gulf of Siam, which was not their true destination to show that they were not heading toward Malaya.

They were indeed spotted that day by a British pilot, who reported that he had seen Japanese warships and transports steaming west 150 miles off the coast of Indochina. That air spotter report reached the desk of Air Chief Marshal Sir Robert Brooke-Popham, who informed General Percival in Kuala Lumpur. Percival put his troops on alert. The Eleventh Indian Division was ordered to be ready to cross into Thailand and, at a moment's notice, move to the three beaches where the British were convinced the Japanese would land.

But the Japanese evasive action had proved successful. The British decided the Japanese were not moving to attack, and they called off the alert shortly afterward.

The convoy steamed on. On December 7, at dusk, a Hudson reconnaissance plane pilot caught sight of four vessels off Singora that looked to him like destroyers. At the same time another British plane spotted the two cruisers.

When this report reached Air Marshal Brooke-Popham he ordered Operation Matador put into effect. But no one moved, and a few hours later the word came that the Japanese warships were shelling the beach at Kota Bharu.

Shortly after midnight, the Japanese transports anchored off Singora. The troop landings began in four- to six-foot seas that threatened to swamp the landing boats. They were met by a patrol from the Thai army, which fired on them with little effect. A few other Thai patrols appeared, but they were soon scattered and beat a hasty retreat into the jungle. The Japanese continued to land until shortly after 5 A.M., when General Yamashita landed and moved into the Singora police headquarters, which had been captured after a brief fight.

By midmorning Yamashita had received word that the diplomats in Bangkok had persuaded the Thai government to give up without further resistance and join the Japanese side of the war effort.

Soon Yamashita had enough news to assess the situation. His landings at Singora had cost only 9 dead and 17 wounded. The landings at Pattani had been unopposed, but at Kota Bharu the British had arrived and fought. One Japanese transport had been sunk by RAF planes, and the Japanese Eighteenth Division was involved in heavy fighting. The Indian troops on the beaches were manning many pillboxes, which held out for hours against determined Japanese attacks. The fighting lasted all night. At dawn Hudson aircraft began to attack the Japanese transports standing offshore.

Then some of the British panicked. The air officer in Singapore received a report that the Kota Bharu airport was under fire by the Japanese. He ordered an immediate evacuation, so all the planes as well as the ground crew left. Then British soldiers at the airfield saw that the Japanese were still more than a mile away, but there was little they could do except destroy the bomb dumps and gasoline supplies.

Now the poor training of the Indian troops began to show. The Hyderabad Infantry Regiment was brought up to protect the airfield, but only a short time into the fighting the commanding officer and his adjutant were killed, and then the troops began to panic. That second afternoon, the Japanese captured the airfield.

The Japanese were also attacking Singapore from the air. The Japanese airfields in Indochina were seven hundred miles away.

"Easy," said Marshal Brooke-Popham. "Our defenses are strong and efficient, and our preparations are made and tested."

But within twenty-four hours the Japanese had captured the airfields at Singora, Pattani, and Kota Bharu. Their planes were bombing Penang and Singapore and supporting the Japanese troops on the line. The Japanese forces were moving forward rapidly. Even so, the Japanese Eighteenth Division lost heavily at Kota Bharu, and Australian aircraft bombed Singora so heavily that corpses and burst bags of rice cluttered the beach.

After two days it was evident the Japanese invasion was succeeding, but their Eighteenth Division was tired. So Yamashita rushed forward the fresh Fifth Division and put the Eighteenth into reserve. The fighting at first was in Thailand. By this time the Thai soldiers were fighting as allies of the Japanese; this hindered the British advance until the Fifth Division could get into action. The British quickly began to realize the Japanese were resourceful and competent soldiers.

Two days after the landings, when the fighting was intense and low morale was a major factor on both sides, something occurred to give the spirits of the Japanese a tremendous boost.

As noted earlier, the British ships *Repulse* and *Prince of Wales* had arrived in Singapore in the early part of December. When the fighting began, Admiral Thomas Phillips on the *Prince of Wales*, decided to take the ships out to find and destroy the Japanese convoy that had apparently moved into the Gulf of Siam. Once out of port, he quickly steamed toward the Anambas Islands, on the Borneo route, because this area was outside the search range of the Japanese. On December 9, Admiral Phillips turned the *Repulse* and the *Prince of Wales* north, toward the Indochina airfields. He believed the Japanese would not find him because they would expect him to be heading toward the Singora and other beaches where the Japanese had landed. He planned to make a sweep to the north and then, at sunset, turn toward those beaches and attack them that night.

"At dawn," said Admiral Phillips, "we shall be to the seaward of Singora and Pattani. I think it is probable that only submarines and enemy aircraft are likely to be sighted."

Admiral Phillips was not aware of the sort of aircraft he was likely to face. He expected army planes, which in the European war had not proved very effective in operations against warships. But the Japanese had an entirely different air system. The navy had its own air arm, which involved not only carriers but a number of land-based air fleets, which had been created because of the nature of the Pacific Ocean with its many islands. To the Japanese an atoll was a permanent carrier, and a land-based air pilot usually had all the skills of a carrier pilot. The navy training program took seven years, which was longer than that of any other country, and the pilots were without a doubt the best in the world.

Unaware of the nature of the Japanese air fleets, the British steamed on. By dusk of December 9 the Japanese had still not found them. But then three Japanese reconnaissance planes spotted the British force.

Admiral Phillips knew he was too close to the Indochinese airfields, and he began a high-speed run toward Singora and the other two beaches, which were about 11 hours away. But the Japanese reconnaissance planes landed near Saigon, and many aircraft which had been loaded with high-explosive bombs destined for Singapore, were quickly rearmed with torpedoes for an attack on the British ships. That night some 25 Japanese planes took off and followed the course they thought Admiral Phillips was pursuing, in an attempt find the British ships so they could attack them under cover of darkness.

At about 8 P.M. Admiral Phillips began having second thoughts and decided to abort the mission and make the run back to Singapore. But then, he decided that he might be in danger of losing his ships if he did, so he headed for the port of Kuantan, halfway between Singapore and Kota Bharu, where it seemed unlikely the Japanese would look for him. He did not realize how competent the Japanese airmen were, nor how hard they had been training for months in the art of searching out enemy carrier groups. This had been one of Yamamoto's major efforts.

At about 8 A.M. Admiral Phillips' ships arrived off Kuantan. Then he headed close inshore up the coast, hoping to make his way to the Japanese beaches and shell them. But by that time, in the broad daylight of December 10, the Japanese were out searching for him. At 10 A.M. he learned that one of his destroyers, off on a decoy mission, was under attack by Japanese aircraft. He turned again and moved out to sea where he would have fighting room.

From everything Admiral Phillips had learned about encounters between aircraft and major capital ships, the balance was on his side. He could expect to hold off the Japanese aircraft until they ran out of fuel and had to return to base. The Japanese had a long way to go, and every plane they diverted to the attack on the ships meant one less to help them on the battlefields.

But Admiral Phillips did not know about what had been happening in the Japanese navy in the past ten years. Under Admiral Yamamoto's guidance, the Japanese had developed the finest naval bombers in the world, and they had the best-trained pilots.

At 10 o'clock on that morning of December 10 one of

the 100 or so bombers that were out searching for the British force found it. In a few minutes the whole search force was alerted, and nearly 90 bombers headed for the British ships. At 11:17 they found the British ships and made their first attack. Some of the bombers were carrying bombs and would attack from high altitude. The others carried torpedoes.

The high-level bombers attacked first. Nine bombers dropped nine bombs, and all of them hit within a hundred feet of their target, the battle cruiser *Repulse*. One landed on the deck. It killed fifty men and started several fires.

Then five torpedo planes attacked the *Prince of Wales*. They came in from five directions; while the ship evaded three of them, two torpedoes struck home. One hit aft, disabling the rudder and cutting the ship's speed from 30 to 15 knots. Another disabled the ship's radio communications, so that thereafter the admiral had to rely on manual communication and word of mouth.

Now came more torpedoes and more bombs. The *Repulse*, which had so far been only bombed, was hit by fifteen torpedo planes, and fourteen of the torpedoes hit. Five minutes later her captain order the ship abandoned, and eight minutes after that the ship sank, taking five hundred men down with her.

Then the *Prince of Wales* was exposed to the full brunt of the Japanese attack and took five more torpedoes. Soon she went down, and Admiral Phillips chose to sink with his ship.

So the Japanese had sunk two of the finest ships of the British navy, with a loss of only three of their own aircraft. Thus came to an end the argument that had raged for years. "Can aircraft sink battleships?" Until this point many admirals had said no. It was ironic that Admiral Tom Phillips, who died that day, was one of the few British admirals who had always said yes.

SIX

Invading the Philippines

The secret of the success of the Japanese invasion of the Philippines, as well as of the Malaya expedition and the victory at Pearl Harbor, was the existence of what was in 1941 the finest naval air force in the world. It was no accident that the Japanese naval air arm was superior. The story of Saburo Sakai, who was to become one of Japan's leading "aces," reveals a good deal about Japanese naval training at that time.

Sakai came from a small town near Sasebo on Kyushu Island. He enlisted in the navy at Sasebo when he was sixteen years old. The year was 1933. The Japanese armed services were just then beginning their drive to catch up with and surpass the Western powers. First, Sakai was subjected to the harsh physical discipline of the Japanese armed services, which was designed to make a man obey, without question, any orders that were given to him.

"They made human cattle of us," he said later, and all his life he never lost his dislike of the petty officers who beat him or the system that tortured him.

This phase of his training was over after six months, and Sakai and his fellow recruits were assigned to duty as apprentice seamen. He was sent to the battleship *Kirishima*. He thought life would be easier in active service, but it was not, and he decided the only way to escape what he considered to be torture was to attain a specialty rating. He began studying aboard ship in his spare time, and in 1935 he passed the entry examination for the navy gunner's school. There he was promoted to seaman and later to petty officer and assigned to the battleship *Haruna*.

So by 1937, the year Japan provoked the "China incident," Petty Officer Sakai had advanced a good deal within the naval service. That year, because of the enormous demands of the services for expansion, he was chosen to become a student pilot at the navy flying school at Tsuchiura, northeast of Tokyo.

The Japanese naval air service was an elite service, drawing its candidates from the Eta Jima naval academy. But by 1937 the need was greater than the supply, and so noncommissioned officers from the ranks were also chosen, as well as a few raw recruits from civil life—but only a few. When Sakai applied in 1937, only 70 noncommissioned officers were selected for pilot training from a list of 1,500 applicants. The navy had not yet begun its enormous expansion campaign that would lead to the creation of "air fleets," or naval commands that operated air forces from island bases.

Pilot training was rigorous, both physically and mentally. First came a month of rigorous physical training, including daily wrestling matches. Then flight lessons began in the mornings, with afternoons devoted to academic courses in weather, navigation, and aeronautics.

The concentration on physical fitness continued and would be maintained all through the training program, because the Japanese naval authorities believed that a pilot had to be superior in every way. For example, one exercise involved training the eyes to discover the stars in the sky during the daylight hours. The instructors told the students that this was important because a fighter plane seen in the sky at a distance of several miles is no easier to identify than a dim star, yet the first pilot to see and recognize the difference between them had an enormous advantage in the fight to come.

It was still the day of the elite. Before the ten-month course was over, 45 of the original 70 noncommissioned officers to apply successfully for the course had failed it and been sent back to other duty. Even on the night before graduation one student was expelled from the school for going to an off-limits bar and drinking. He was guilty of two unpardonable offenses: he had drunk alcohol on the night before a flight, and he had entered an institution marked off-limits.

At the end of 1937, Sakai and 24 other noncommissioned officers were graduated and became full-fledged naval pilots. Immediately they were committed to advanced training, which included carrier training, although most of these pilots, including Sakai, would never fly from a carrier during the war but would be assigned to land bases in the various islands.

In May 1938, Sakai's war began, with operations at the air base at Kiukiang in southeastern China. At first he flew low-level strafing missions in support of the Japanese army on the ground, but soon he was flying fighter missions, designed to intercept Chinese fighters and bombers, over the China front around Hankow. They were flying Mitsubishi 96-type fighter planes with fixed wheels, a plane later given the nickname Claude by the Americans.

In 1939 Sakai was back in Japan, training again. Then he was transferred to Taiwan. And here at Aohsiung airfield, he met the Zero fighter, which was to be Japan's finest in the early years of the Pacific war. He participated in the occupation of Indochina. Then he was assigned again to the central China front and flew missions along the Yangtze River until the fall of 1941, when he was again transferred. This time, he and his fellow pilots were informed of the transfer by Vice Admiral Eikichi Katagiri, the naval air force commander in China. They were very lucky, said the admiral. They had been chosen to fulfill a most important mission elsewhere. Soon they were on Taiwan, organized at Taiwan airfield as the new Tainan Air Flotilla. And they were waiting.

On December 2, 1941, Vice Admiral Fushizo Tsukahara, the commander of the Eleventh Air Fleet, began the operations against the American enemy in the Philippines with the dispatch of reconnaissance planes to Luzon Island.

By December 5 the recon planes had gathered full information about the Clark and other airfield complexes. They had taken aerial photographs from 20,000 feet and had been unobserved. The calculated that there were 32 B–17 heavy bombers in the Clark Field complex and that at Nichols Field and others, there were about 300 warplanes of various types. Actually their estimates were high.

Originally the Japanese attack plan for the Philippines had called for the use of three light carriers, but when the navy began its final planning, Admiral Tsukahara found that the three carriers were really inadequate for the task. He and his staff devised a plan to use the new Zero fighters with long-range gas tanks to make the 1,000-mile round trip from Taiwan to the Manila area and return. This plan was extremely daring, since the average range of military fighters in those days was about 350 miles. True, the Zero was light and had a long range, but it had a gas-tank capacity of only 180 gallons, which would keep it in the air for some six or seven hours. The flight to the Philippines would require far more time.

So the pilots began training for long-range missions, where the idea was to keep fuel consumption to a minimum. They perfected the technique so that they were able to stay aloft from 10 to 12 hours.

At 2 A.M on December 8, 1941, the pilots of the Eleventh Air Fleet on Taiwan were awakened and hurried to the briefing place where they were told they would take off at 4 A.M. They went to wait next to their planes. Breakfast was brought to them there. They ate sitting on the ground and then began to grow a little nervous as fog closed in on the airstrip. By 4 A.M. it was so thick operations had to be delayed.

Time went by, but it was still too foggy to take off. At 6 A.M. the pilots were informed over the loudspeaker of the attack on Pearl Harbor, and they raised a cheer, although many of them realized this meant they would face strong opposition from aroused Americans in the Philippines.

At 9 A.M. the fog finally lifted, and the planes took off at 10. One bomber crashed on the runway when its landing gear failed on takeoff; the bomb load blew up and all the crew were killed. But the runway was quickly cleared by ground crews, and the rest of the bombers and fighters took off and at 10:45 were on their way toward Manila.

The attackers were split into two groups. One would first conduct a fighter sweep to scour the airfields and hit any planes trying to take off. This was to be followed a few minutes later by the Japanese bombers with their fighter escort.

At 1:35 in the afternoon, the first Japanese planes crossed the Philippine coastline and headed for Clark Field. Since they had heard of the Pearl Harbor attack, the Japanese pilots had been worrying about an attack from the Americans and expected the Americans to be in the air to meet them. But when they arrived at Clark Field they found about 150 American fighters and bombers standing neatly in rows on the field below. They did see five American fighter planes in the air, but the Americans did not attack, and the Japanese were ordered not to start their attack until their bombers arrived.

At 1:45 the bombers arrived, nearly 30 of them, with their Zero escorts. The fighters swept down, but no enemy fighters came up to intercept them. The bombers dropped their bombs; when they were finished the field was a burning mess. The fighters then finished off the attack with strafing. Some American P–40 fighters made a pass but were immediately outclassed. Four of them fled; the fifth was shot down over the field. The Japanese then went back to Taiwan. When they landed they discovered the single casualty of the day was the plane that had blown up on the runway on takeoff. The attack had been perfect as far as the Tainan contingent was concerned. Elsewhere, the Japanese lost about half a dozen planes that day.

On December 9 the Japanese air force returned to attack the Philippines again but with little result. The weather was bad, and the bombers stayed home. The fighter planes found little to shoot at; the American air forces had been nearly knocked out in that first violent raid. On the third day, December 10, the Japanese were back again, and this time they found some aircraft, about 20 B–17 bombers, that had managed to escape the first attack by taking off and flying south.

The reason for the December 10th Japanese air attack was to protect their convoy, which was landing invasion troops at Vigan. Four transports and a half dozen warships were in the convoy. Some American B–17s came in very high and dropped bombs but couldn't hit anything from such a high altitude; then they streaked off. The Japanese fighter planes were a long way below them.

The major damage done to the Americans in the Philippines on December 10 was at Cavite, as a result of the Japanese attack on the navy base there. Some 50 bombers cruised in at 20,000 feet, which was outside the range of the Americans' old-fashioned three-inch antiaircraft guns, and bombed as they pleased. The bombing was very accurate, and soon the whole navy yard was ablaze. So was most of the town of Cavite. The one bright spot for the Americans was the failure of the enemy to hit the navy ammunition depot.

But by nightfall in the rest of the navy yard, the fires were still raging, and the American defenders had to admit that they were out of control. That night Admiral Hart ordered as many stores and as much ammunition as possible were to be saved, and the sailors began moving what they could to Corregidor and Sangley Point.

That same day, the Japanese also bombed the submarine *Sealion* and the minesweeper *Bittern* in the harbor. Worse than that was the destruction of more than 200 torpedoes in the navy yard. The Americans would feel that loss for a long time.

This was the day that Admiral Glassford's gunboats arrived. The *Mindanao* came in. Of course, the gunboats were of virtually no use in a modern war; they had been devised to patrol China's rivers in the days of the warlords, and their armaments and configuration was such as to make them virtually sitting ducks in an air attack.

From December 10 the war took on a much grimmer aspect for the Americans. The Japanese had been troubled by the Catalina flying boats that had coursed over Taiwan in the earlier days of the war, and they sent a squadron of Zeros to Manila Bay. The Zeros found the Catalinas at their moorings and sank all of them.

Admiral Hart divided his ships and sent them out of Manila to avoid air attack. Admiral Glassford, when he arrived from China, was put in charge of the "striking force" Hart wanted to use to attack the Japanese amphibious forces that were moving on the Philippines. But with the destruction of the American land-based air force, the Japanese had control of the air; it obviously became impossible to send the surface ships up to brave such an attack. So the Japanese came in at will.

The first Japanese landings had been made on Bataan in the Bashi Channel on December 8 before the first attack on the Philippines. This was a precautionary move, to have Japanese in control of the rear, so that if one of their planes had engine trouble during the attacks, there would be somewhere to put down. In fact, however, there was no need to use the Bataan base that day. On December 10 the force that had occupied Bataan moved over to Camiguin Island and established a seaplane base there.

The second Japanese landing in the Philippines came at Aparri on the northern coast of Luzon Island. For such operations the Japanese used special task forces, usually about the size of a reinforced battalion and made up of troops trained specially for storming operations. This force was known as the Tanaka detachment, after its commander.

The Tanaka detachment had left Taiwan on December 7 and landed at Aparri on December 10. There was opposition by a single company of the U.S. Eleventh Infantry Division. The Japanese were much more troubled by the weather, which became stormy and permitted the landing of only two companies of the Tanaka detachment that day. The transports moved out of the stormy area to a point 20 miles east, which was protected by Cape Engano.

The storm was not the only difficulty the Japanese faced. On the first day American P–40 fighters and half a dozen B–17 bombers attacked the Japanese landing force at Aparri and blew up minesweeper No. 19. This loss made the Japanese task force commander nervous, and he ordered the transports to hurry up with their unloading. The crews jettisoned the drums of oil that were supposed to be landed and let them drift ashore. Some heavy equipment meant to be used on airfields was not unloaded at all, and if the Americans had been able to put another battalion of troops and more planes in the air, they could have defeated the Japanese landing. But as it was the Japanese had the Aparri airstrip under control by lunchtime on the first day. Then they discovered that this airstrip and the one at Camaluniuguan, a few miles to the south, were completely unsuitable for use by bombers. So the plans had to be changed and delayed and a new airfield found 50 miles away.

The Tanaka battalion had expected to have air support from bombers operating out of the Luzon airfields but did not get it. Even so, the detachment found the opposition on the ground so slight that it moved very swiftly to the Cagayan River valley and headed south toward Manila.

The Japanese were extremely lucky because the Americans suddenly began to discover that what they thought was their single most effective weapon in the Philippines was turning out to be a dud. This was the submarine force. The fault did not lie with the men who sailed the submarines but with the men who had designed the American submarine torpedoes.

At the end of World War I, the Americans, who occupied Germany along with the British and the French, were much impressed by the progress made by the German navy in torpedo development. Indeed, the Americans brought home examples of the German torpedoes and copied them, including their exploder mechanisms. The German design then became the prototype for the American torpedo. But of course no torpedoes were fired in anger from 1919 until 1941. The American torpedoes worked all right in practice, with dummy warheads, as did the German prototype. But what the Germans and the Americans both learned as they began World War II was that the German-developed exploder mechanism was faulty, and the torpedoes of both nations failed as often or more often than they succeeded. Admiral Doenitz, the German submarine commander, learned this sad lesson in the spring of 1940 during the Norwegian campaign, when his submarines were supposed to do great damage to the British fleet and failed completely. The Americans began to learn the same lesson on December 14, 1941, when the U.S. submarine *Seawolf* torpedoed the Japanese transport *Sanyo Maru*—and the ship did not even falter. The torpedo was a dud.

The next Japanese landing was scheduled for Pandan, three miles southeast of Vigan. On December 10, General Nishimura sent the 4,400 troops of the landing force ashore, or at least he started to, but the American air force intervened and the weather acted up. The Americans sank minesweeper No. 10, strafed the admiral's flagship, and damaged two transports so badly they had to be run up on the beach and left there. The amphibious force encountered found so much difficulty in landing that the troops and ships were moved down to Santa, where they landed the following day.

Next came the landing at Legaspi, south of Manila and not far from San Bernardino Strait, which separates Luzon

Island from Samar. This was an important operation because of the significance of the strait. It was protected by a Japanese task force, while another large Japanese force laid mines in San Bernardino Strait and Surigao Strait to prevent the Americans from reinforcing these areas.

On December 14, the American air force sent five B–17 bombers to attack the Japanese ships anchored in Legaspi harbor. They did not sink any ships with their high-level bombing, but one B–17 came down low and its gunners strafed a minesweeper. Then the B–17 was jumped by Zero fighters and barely got back to its base; its radio operator was dead, two crewmen were wounded, two of the four engines were knocked out, and it was full of hundreds of bullet holes. The fact that it was able to land was a great tribute to the Boeing aircraft company engineers.

The Legaspi operation was the last for the B–17s. There were only 14 left in the Far East, and the handwriting was on the wall. There was no fighter cover for them, and there were too many Japanese fighter planes in the sky. So on December 17 the 14 Flying Fortresses took off for Darwin, Australia, where they would regroup and become the nucleus of General George Kenney's Fifth Air Force, which would soon join the long fight against Japan.

The Japanese had unloaded their landing forces at Bataan, Aparri, and Vigan and had sent the ships back to Taiwan and the Pescadores to pick up more troops of the main landing force for the Philippines. Warships that had been covering the landings on the Malayan shore were now diverted to the Philippines to cover these new landings. They were really not needed; the Americans had nothing like the Japanese naval forces in the area to oppose the landings successfully. Vice Admiral Kondo's Distant Cover Force alone, consisting of two battleships and two heavy cruisers, completely overpowered the whole American Asiatic Fleet except for the submarines, and, as noted, the submarines were having their own troubles.

The major Japanese landing forces were heading for Lingayen Gulf. On December 18 the Japanese naval air force, now using the new Japanese air bases at Aparri and Vigan, struck the defenses at Lingayen. The amphibious landing convoy was completely unopposed by the Americans at sea or in the air. It arrived offshore on the night of December 21.

Admiral Hart ordered American submarines to go into Lingayen Gulf and attack the landing convoy. Lieutenant W. G. Chapple in *S–38* did manage to get in close and sank the transport *Hayo Maru* on December 22. The USS *Seal* sank the freighter *Hayataka Maru*. The seaplane tender *Sanuki Maru* was damaged by fire from American shore batteries. But the Japanese had been prepared for real naval opposition, and when it did not appear except as noted above, the admirals were delighted with the results.

The Japanese landings began at dawn on December 22, accompanied by air cover that included fighter strikes at American military encampments and Clark Field. A few American fighters did get into the air and strafed some ships, but the damage was minimal and the landings were not affected.

The Japanese Forty-eighth Division landed near San Fernando Point. Because of a mix-up the Japanese fighter cover failed to arrive, and once ashore the troops found themselves attacked by American army planes and PBY patrol bombers. Still, the main difficulty for the Japanese was the weather—stormy, with high tides, which kept them from landing their heavy equipment.

So the Forty-eighth Division landed and began moving down Luzon Island. Two days later the Japanese Sixteenth Division landed at Lamon Bay on the east coast of Luzon, very close to Manila. There was no opposition, and the troops began marching over the mountains toward Manila, joined by the shock troops of the Legaspi force.

General MacArthur had word of the landings and knew that without an air force and with very limited infantry forces, he had no chance of stopping a Japanese attack on Manila, so he announced that Manila would become an open city and evacuated. He planned to move into the Bataan

Peninsula, the area where he would stage the defense of the Philippines.

To the Japanese the southern Philippines area was much more important than Manila and Luzon, because Mindanao Island was very close to Borneo and its vital oil fields. So a much larger force was sent to this area, including an aircraft carrier, the *Ryujo,* and a seaplane tender, the *Chitose*. This force escorted thousands of Japanese troops bound for Davao. The first day, the Japanese established a seaplane base in Talomo Bay, south of Davao. The American airfields in the area were swiftly occupied, and the Eleventh Air Fleet moved planes down from Taiwan to create a land-based air force on Mindanao.

The American naval strike force, which had left Cavite on the night of the first Japanese air raid, headed for Balikpapan. Almost immediately Admiral Hart also sent three submarine tenders south to join Admiral Glassford. As the American gunboats arrived from China waters, they, too, were sent down, eventually arriving at Java. Several destroyers had been left at Manila, but when General MacArthur evacuated the city, Admiral Hart decided to send the destroyers to join the forces converging on Java. One of them, the *Peary,* after many close escapes from Japanese attack, finally made its way to Australia. The *Pillsbury,* which left at the same time, had an uneventful voyage before she joined Admiral Glassford's command.

One by one the handful of ships of the American Asiatic Fleet made their way south to get away from the attacking Japanese. At noon on Christmas Day 1941, Admiral Hart turned over command of all American naval forces in the Philippines to Rear Admiral F. W. Rockwell. Admiral Hart had planned to escape from the Philippines by PBY, but the PBYs, which were hidden in a mangrove swamp, were discovered by Japanese search planes and destroyed. So Admiral Hart boarded the submarine *Shark* with his staff and left early on the morning of December 26 for Java, where the British, Dutch, and Americans had vowed to make a stand against the Japanese invaders.

After General MacArthur's command moved to Bataan, under the war plan approved by the military authorities in Washington, War Plan Orange No. 3 was to be implemented. What a plan it was! It called for the Americans to hold on at Bataan with a garrison of about 40,000 men for six months until an American relief expedition could be organized. But in Washington there was no plan for relief, and the navy estimated it would take them two years to ready a force to send to the Philippines. So the reality was that although MacArthur, as an aggressive fighter, wanted to use the three divisions of American troops to fight the Japanese to the water's edge, with at least a strong relief air force backing him up, America had already decided to abandon the Philippines to their fate.

With the Lingayen landings the Japanese planned a double envelopment of the Americans on Luzon. They did not expect the Americans to move so swiftly into the Bataan Peninsula. General Honma planned to use the Forty-eighth and Sixteenth divisions for this purpose, and they were already converging on Manila from two directions. But Lieutenant General Susumu Morioka's One hundred-sixteenth Infantry had already sacrificed the Thirty-third Infantry in the landings. The Forty-eighth Infantry had lost the Second Formosan Regiment. So Honma's Fourteenth Army had only 35,000 men, which was just slightly smaller than the American defense forces. This was characteristic of the whole Japanese strike south; in every case, the Imperial Army used far fewer troops than the enemy expected, and in every case they had so far been so lucky that Imperial General Headquarters was beginning to expect their luck to be the norm.

The Fourteenth Army, under the Japanese war plan, was given 50 days in which to complete operations in the Philippines. Then the major assault forces, including the Forty-

eighth Infantry, would move south to participate in the struggle for the Dutch East Indies.

On December 24, Brigadier General George M. Parker,
who had been conducting the South Luzon defense, was
relieved and given the task of organizing the Bataan Defense
Force.

On Christmas Day the Americans began to move—the
Thirty-first Infantry Division, the Forty-first Infantry Division, the Seventy-first Infantry Division, and Twenty-sixth
Cavalry. Between December 28 and December 30 the Japanese advanced, but the Americans carried out a planned
withdrawal, whose success was evident by the few prisoners
that were taken by the advancing Japanese. General Honma
was mopping up as he went, establishing clear communications and control, but the Americans were moving steadily
toward Bataan, and the battle was not nearly over yet.

General Honma made a serious miscalculation at this
point. He and his staff failed to recognize the fact that they
had won all the way, but not one of the encounters was a
battle. The Americans had scattered before them. Perhaps
it was egotistic, the Japanese belief that no one could stand
up against the Imperial Army, but Honma failed to recognize
the nature of the American retreat into Bataan and thus made
no attempt to block it; the American vehicles were backed
up for miles at bridges and junctions, but the Japanese air
force made no attacks. The two bridges across the Pampanga
River at Calumpit were vital; had the Japanese blown them
up the Americans would not have been able to retreat from
southern Luzon into Bataan, but the Japanese considered
the bridges too small to waste bombs on them. And so
virtually all the American southern Luzon force made its
way in orderly retreat to the Bataan Peninsula.

The Americans withdrew and the Japanese moved along
two main routes that came together at Calamba on the southern shore of Laguna de Bay. The Americans blew up installations and withdrew. The Japanese advanced. On Route
1 the Japanese tried to encircle the Fifty-first Infantry Division and failed. They did threaten two American battalions

of the First Infantry Regiment on December 27, but as the year drew to a close, some 14,000 of the 15,000 American defenders of south Luzon made their way into the Bataan Peninsula and temporary safety.

On January 2, the Japanese marched into Manila. With that news, Count Terauchi, the commander of the southern army at Saigon, ordered the Forty-eighth Army south to join in the assault on the Dutch East Indies.

When Imperial General Headquarters issued that order, the general staff knew that it might prolong the Philippine campaign, but they did not, at that time, care. The capture of the Philippines, in a strategic sense, was relatively unimportant or, one might say, important only because it would drive the Americans out of Asia. The Dutch Indies were important because they held the resources Japan needed for war and peace—oil, minerals, and food.

Further, because of their experience so far, the Japanese did not expect the Americans to put up a serious fight in the Philippines. Imperial General Headquarters was beginning to believe its own propaganda—that the Westerners were effete cowards who would not and could not stand up to the imperial forces.

In the first few days of January 1942, the Americans from northern Luzon, and the Filipinos who were fighting with them, tried to escape to Bataan as well. After a series of engagements with the Japanese, 15,000 troops did escape and joined the 65,000 troops and 26,000 civilians already on the peninsula.

So, as of January 6, the war of movement in the Philippines had ended. The Japanese controlled the islands and could move their troops at will. The Americans who had not reached Bataan had either been captured or killed or had moved out into the countryside to become guerillas. The main American force now controlled the Bataan Peninsula and the Corregidor fortress and were prepared for a siege. It now began.

SEVEN

Bataan

Down in the Dutch East Indies, in the last days of December 1941, the fighting force of the American Asiatic Fleet—Task Force 5—was getting ready to battle the enemy under conditions that the staff hoped would give them a chance of victory. Admiral Glassford set up an advanced headquarters at Surabaya. He and chief of staff Admiral Purnell made trips up to Batavia to see Vice Admiral C. E. L. Helfrich, the Dutch commander of Allied naval forces in the Dutch East Indies. There they met the senior British officer, Commodore John Collins. They worked out a plan that called for the Americans to protect the area between Borneo and the Celebes Islands, including Makassar and the Molucca straits and extending east into the Banda Sea that abuts New Guinea.

The British would protect the area between Singapore and Sarawak, while the Dutch had the whole Java Sea to protect.

It was not easy for three different navies with three different ways of doing things to work together. The Americans, for example, had 1,300 miles of shoreline to protect, and they had no charts of the area. The Dutch had charts, but not enough of them, so they hand traced the charts to give the Americans copies. No, it was not easy.

* * *

Admiral Glassford had the most unenviable of positions. Soon to join him would be Admiral Hart, who did not like Glassford. And from Washington came a steady stream of complaints from Admiral King, who wanted—needed—some sort of victory, something to shore up the American morale after the recent steady stream of disasters. To that end Admiral King was demanding some sort of naval action "to give the American people a much needed victory." Admiral Glassford was ready to grasp at straws, and he did. At Townsville, on the northeast coast of Australia, he learned of the existence of an army installation with a squadron of 21 American planes. The planes were all brand-new, still in the crates that had brought them from America. The pilots were also all brand-new, recent graduates of flight school. It was agreed between the army and navy that the fighter squadron would bring the planes north to the Indies and fight there.

The squadron took off from Townsville. At each stop one or two planes crashed because of the incompetence of the pilots. More were lost in the over-water routes between islands. Finally, five planes—all that was left of the squadron—arrived in Java, in such terrible condition that not one of them ever flew in combat. It seemed that Admiral Glassford was expected to fight the powerful Japanese military machine with equipment and untrained personnel like these.

As the end of the month neared it was apparent that the skies above Manila Bay were now Japanese skies, so Admiral Hart moved every vessel that could be taken out of the bay to join Admiral Glassford in the south. On December 26, the two destroyers *Peary* and *Pillsbury,* which had been held to do odd jobs for Admiral Hart, were attacked by 50 Japanese planes, so Hart decided it was time for them to leave. They were dispatched to Balikpapan to join Glassford's Task Force No. 5. The *Pillsbury* made the voyage uneventfully, but the *Peary* had an adventure that indicated the state of things in the southern hemisphere just then.

The *Peary* had already been blooded in the war. She had been bombed first on December 10 when the Japanese attacked Cavite for the first time. Her captain had been wounded, and the ship had been put under the command of Lieutenant Commander John L. Bermingham.

On the night of December 26 the *Peary* sailed for Balikpapan. On the morning of December 27 she anchored at Campomanes Bay on the island of Negros, halfway down the Philippine chain. There Skipper Bermingham stopped to camouflage the ship to break up the gray lines that would so quickly identify her. The crew went ashore and brought back tree branches, and the captain found some green paint.

While they were anchored there the crew saw five Japanese bombers passing overhead at high altitude, but the planes did not hesitate or indicate that they had seen the ship. Still, there was a chance they had radioed back to their base, so Bermingham decided to move the ship. In an hour she was moving to Asia Bay. At Asia Bay the camouflage job was completed as best the crew could manage.

That afternoon the *Peary* sailed for the south to skirt around Mindanao. She steamed along at 25 knots until the morning of December 28, when she passed Jolo Island and entered the Celebes Sea. All went well until the ship's crew spotted a big, four-engined Kawanishi flying boat, a plane used by the Japanese as a bomber and long-range observation plane. The Kawanishi headed for the *Peary* as if to attack, so Captain Bermingham maneuvered sharply, managing to keep away from the flying boat. Ultimately the pilot grew tired of the game and dropped back, but he continued to shadow the *Peary* all day long.

A dispatch from Task Force No. 5 indicated that a Japanese submarine was laying mines in Makassar Strait and that an enemy cruiser was working off northern Borneo. Captain Bermingham changed course so as to avoid both, then radioed that he was being shadowed by a Kawanishi.

That afternoon two more flying boats were sighted, but when they approached, it was apparent they were not Kawanishis but PBYs. Since they did not respond to signals, Captain Bermingham concluded they were Dutch patrol bombers, and so he held his guns silent as they passed aloft and flew away. Then three more Kawanishi flying boats joined the shadower, and the four launched an attack on the destroyer.

The Kawanishis were dropping 250-kilogram bombs, but they were not very accurate. Or perhaps it was that Commander Bermingham kept them guessing, spinning figure eights and circles and wavy lines in the sea, moving the ship this way and that to confuse the bombardiers.

He did a good job; not one of the bombs dropped by the Kawanishis on two runs struck home. But then the captain saw, low on the horizon, a torpedo plane and then another, streaking in to attack. Both dropped their torpedoes; the *Peary* turned and the torpedoes missed. Then one of the Kawanishis sneaked up and tried to hit the *Peary,* but the captain ordered emergency speed, and the ship, which had come to a stop after turning, went from zero to 15 knots in a few seconds. The Kawanishi dropped four bombs, all of which missed, a hundred yards astern.

Then the *Peary* was beset again by the torpedo planes; this time they were strafing. The *Peary* fired back with 30-caliber machine guns, 50-caliber machine guns, and her four-inch guns.

Skipper Bermingham moved the ship through the Banka Strait at the northeast tip of Celebes Island. That evening three Lockheed Hudson bombers showed up, looking for a Japanese task force that had just moved into the Menado area, a few miles away. One of the bomber pilots thought the *Peary* was a Japanese ship and attacked the destroyer. The bomb missed, but it knocked one seaman overboard. There was no way the ship could be stopped to pick him up. Someone threw a life jacket overboard, and when last seen, the seaman was swimming for it.

Then all three Hudsons dropped bombs on the destroyer, but fortunately none of them connected. There was another near miss, just 10 yards off the port propeller. Shrapnel scattered around the ship, and fragments cut the steam supply line to the steering engine; another piece of shrapnel killed a seaman manning a 30-caliber machine gun.

Captain Bermingham reported the attack by radio, and the report was picked up by the land base of the Hudson bombers. When they arrived at their base, their explanation was that they had believed the destroyer was being convoyed by the four Kawanishi flying boats, so of course they had assumed she was Japanese.

That night the *Peary*'s weary crew moored at Maitara Island in the Halmahera group, with lines strung from bow and stern to coconut trees ashore. The crew then looked over the ship for damage. The most damage was to the starboard engine, which was now out of commission. The ship was also short of fuel; it had only 19,000 gallons of oil left. According to the chief engineer, this would be just enough to get them to Ambon on one engine. The next day they left for Ambon, where they arrived on December 31, took on more fuel, had the starboard engine repaired, and then moved on to Darwin, Australia, where they arrived on January 3.

Admiral Hart had released the seaplane tender *Heron* to join Admiral Glassford, because all the PBYs in the Philippines were now gone. Since there were so many Japanese task forces steaming around the Philippines, the skipper of the *Heron* was instructed to make his way alone down to Balikpapan. She was steaming as ordered on the morning of December 31 when one of the Kawanishi flying boats now based in the southern Philippines sighted her and attacked with 100-pound bombs. The bomber struck twice but missed with all bombs, and the *Heron* moved on through a squall. But behind her, tailing and watching, came the big Kawanishi. Soon other Japanese planes, four-engined Kawanishis and twin-engined bombers, came in to attack. One bomb smashed the *Heron*'s mainmast. Another destroyed the three-inch gun on the port side. The attacks lasted all day long. By late afternoon, when more Japanese planes appeared, the men of the *Heron* were exhausted. Some of the planes launched torpedoes, some bombed, some strafed. The *Heron* fielded all attacks and shot down one

Kawanishi. Then the *Heron* steamed on, ultimately reaching safety at Balikpapan.

Admiral Glassford had one good break. On his way from China back to Washington, Army Air Corps Lieutenant General G. H. Brett stopped off at Surabaya and met with Glassford, who registered his complaint about the paucity of air power. Brett promised to try to do something, and he did. Soon after he went to Australia a whole squadron of B–17 bombers appeared at Surabaya.

At this time the Japanese were gearing up for action in the Indies. They took Sarawak in northwest Borneo and captured Kuching. They lost men and some ships; the destroyers *Nojima, Sagiri,* and *Murasame* were all casualties either of enemy attack or of grounding in shallow water.

The British—using too little too late—were moving to try to stop the Japanese. Air Chief Marshal Brooke-Popham was relieved of his command, and Sir Archibald Wavell was put in charge of British forces in the southwest Pacific area. He moved his headquarters to Java, because it was obvious by the end of 1941 that the Japanese juggernaut would soon descend on Singapore.

On New Year's Eve, General Yamashita put into effect a plan that would hasten that event. He had brought with him from Hainan Island forty landing craft and a number of portable motorboats. Yamashita decided to employ a battalion of his infantry, a section of mountain guns, and a section of engineers to outflank the enemy. The members of his staff, particularly Lieutenant Colonel Tsuji, opposed this idea. It was too dangerous, they said; the little flotilla would be annihilated by the British naval forces patrolling off the coasts. This argument reinforced the bad relations between Yamashita and Tsuji, and the colonel soon went off to the Philippines to report to Imperial Headquarters that Yamashita was a troublesome person.

Having overruled Tsuji, Yamashita ordered 1,500 men to land south of the British forces. But Colonel Tsuji had transmitted his arguments to the colonel in charge of this operation, and that colonel had agreed that the mission was too dangerous. Thus, when the force sighted a single British patrol plane, the colonel stopped moving down the coast to his objective and pulled in at the nearest river. Because of this action, only 100 of the 1,500 men sent to outflank the British actually arrived at the proper point. They found themselves alone and so went back to join the others. When the Japanese landing party was sighted by the British, the British did not know what to make of this force and assumed it was some major unit that had just been sent into action in the mangrove swamps. So the British moved faster in their retreat.

The Fifth Division drove down the road near the capital of Kuala Lumpur. Four hundred yards away, through the jungle, ran the railroad.

The British decided to make a stand at the Slim River. There the Japanese landed in two waves. Their motorboats carried them across the river. Japanese tanks rumbled up and down the road. The British placed a 4.5-inch howitzer behind some concrete blocks. When the leading Japanese tank was only 25 yards away the British howitzer fired and the Japanese tank burst into flames. The Japanese crew tried to get out but were machine-gunned. The ruined Japanese tank blocked the road, but the Japanese infantry fanned out on both sides of the road and cleared a way for the other Japanese tanks. The British fought back. The battle lasted 19 hours before the Japanese routed them and began to move down the road once again. The rout was complete; survivors were so confused that no one went ahead to inform head-quarters that the Japanese had broken through their defenses and were racing down the road.

Soon the Japanese tanks, bicycle troops, and infantry were 10 miles behind the British lines. The first the British rear echelon learned of this was when two battalions of British infantry marched up the road to join the Slim River battle and were met and decimated by the Japanese before they could get off the road.

The Japanese captured 54 British field guns, 50 armored

cars, and 1,500 vehicles of other sorts. They took 1,200 prisoners; a little later another 2,000 men came out of the jungle to surrender. Yamashita had no more concerns about supplies; he had enough captured British supplies to keep his troops going for a month. On their part, as a result of the battle of the Slim River, the British decided to abandon Kuala Lumpur.

Yamashita was not pleased with the performance of the Fifth Division even though it had won the battle, so he decided to use the Imperial Guards Division to carry out his boat landings and infiltration. This plan worked so well that the British were forced to speed up their general retreat.

Yamashita also decided he no longer needed the Fifty-sixth Division and told field Marshal Terauchi that division could be sent to Burma to help with the invasion there.

Yamashita forged ahead toward Singapore. The British were confused; their troop traffic became so jammed that 13 trains were shunted onto sidings at Kuala Lumpur and abandoned there. Most of the trains carried new equipment and supplies for the British, which the Japanese would now be able to use, including new maps of Singapore that had been meant for the British in that city. The Japanese now had the maps, and the British had none as the Japanese approached the city.

The British now pulled back to Johore, the state adjoining Singapore Island. They planned to bring all their troops into Singapore and then destroy the Johore causeway. In Singapore they would make their stand.

For the Japanese, the last obstacle before Singapore was the Muar River with its road and rail bridge. The river was 600 yards wide. The land south of the river was rubber plantations and rice fields, which meant easy going for the Japanese troops. On January 18, the Japanese sent two divisions down the road toward the Muar.

By the end of December 1941, the people who remained in Manila were waiting for the end. The men who could fight were either gone or would soon be going to the Bataan

Peninsula to join the British soldiers there. The women and children would have to take what the Japanese meted out to them. There was no place for them in Bataan, no way that noncombatants could be accommodated there.

The Japanese were bombing the port facilities at Cavite and other areas almost every day. They hit the radio towers and Sangley Point. As of December 19 U.S. naval operations had moved to Queen Tunnel on the fortress island of Corregidor, and the installations at Cavite and Sangley Point were destroyed. Someone there remembered too late that the officer who had been in charge of destruction of the mines stored at Sangley Point had not blown them up, and Lieutenant Malcolm Champlin volunteered for the job. He took 25 volunteers, most of them men who—before the Japanese attack—had been confined to the brig for various breaches of discipline, and a motor launch. He commandeered the salvage ship *Pigeon,* and as darkness fell on December 19, they headed for Sangley Point. One group of men was sent to find cars and bring them to move men and materiel. Another group would move the mines.

At Sangley Point Champlin encountered an American engineer who had a force of 100 Filipino laborers with him and commandeered them. Champlin then went into Cavite City where he saw the mayor, who told him that the Japanese had come and gone. They had brought a tank into Cavite City, but they soon realized the Americans were gone. The Japanese officer in charge feared the place was mined, so he and his men had left the city.

Lieutenant Champlin moved around Sangley Point leading the last American crew. They blew up gasoline dumps and destroyed airplane engines left by Pan American Airways personnel at their shop. They destroyed the damaged PBY aircraft that had been left there by Patrol Wing 10 of the naval air force, when it had pulled out for Borneo.

For two more days the Americans destroyed what they had brought to the Philippines so the enemy would not be able to use it, and they towed the mines out to sea and dumped them in deep water.

In the last few days the navy mined Subic Bay, hoping to surprise a Japanese ship or two.

On Christmas Eve, Lieutenant Champlin learned that civilian oil supplies had not been destroyed, and he took a crew out to burn them. They spent Christmas Eve watching bonfires burning, burning, burning.

December 25, Christmas Day. This was the day that Hong Kong finally fell to the Japanese, and the world had its first knowledge of the sort of treatment that would be meted out to the white man in Asia by the victorious Japanese. Japanese troops invaded hospitals, bayoneted the patients, killed the doctors and orderlies, and raped the nurses. None of this, of course, was reported back home to the people of Japan; rather, the idea that the Japanese army was invincible and that Japanese people were a master race was being spread to Japan and the rest of the world. In view of the string of victories by Japanese, many defeatists the world over began to believe what the Japanese propagandists were saying.

"The Anglo-Saxon influence is rapidly waning and in its place a rapid rise is being witnessed in the Asiatic countries. The war of Greater East Asia will create a new and glorious page in the history of the world," said a propaganda article prepared for the Japanese newspapers.

In the Philippines, even the American submarines were moved out at the end of the year. Captain Wilkes, the commander, went to Surabaya to set up a base. Commander James Fife was ordered to Darwin to establish a permanent seaplane base and departed in the submarine *Seawolf*.

General MacArthur moved onto Bataan Peninsula to set up the defense of the Philippines as the year 1941 came to an end.

On December 26, Admiral Rockwell, who had moved to Corregidor, paid an official call on General MacArthur, who had moved from his Manila office building to the Corregidor fortress to direct the defense of Bataan. That day the navy also moved everything movable to Mariveles, at the foot of the peninsula and near Corregidor. All remaining naval vessels were also clustered in the lee of Monkey Point, on the southeast shore of Corregidor. There the guns of the fortress could offer them some defense against air attack.

The Japanese had it all their own way in the air as well as on the ground. On December 28 the American submarine tender *Canopus* was bombed even though she was camouflaged. On December 29 the Japanese began their bombing of Corregidor, and *Canopus* was bombed again. This time 25 men were killed in the attack.

On December 30 the town of Mariveles was bombed and set afire.

On December 31 the army troops consolidated their defenses on Bataan and made ready for the Japanese attack, which they expected at any hour.

The Japanese siege of Bataan began on January 7, 1942.

The Japanese in the Philippines, buoyed by news of their successes on all other fronts and by their own easy successes in Luzon, expected a quick victory over the Americans. The Americans, knowing that they had not yet lost a battle and understanding that they now occupied a strong position, were eager to come to grips with the enemy, confident that help would soon be arriving from the United States.

The Bataan Peninsula was ideal for defense. The terrain was steep, mountainous, and mostly covered by thick jungle. Only on the eastern coastal plain would the Japanese be able to use tanks. The thick jungle offered good concealment and would hamper Japanese aircraft.

The Americans chose an area between Mauban and Mabatang as their main line of resistance. Their secondary defense line, the rear battle position, lay across the road from Bagac and Orion.

Major General Jonathan M. Wainwright commanded the First Philippine Corps, which consisted of the First, the Twenty-first, and Ninety-first divisions, as well as the Twenty-sixth Cavalry.

General Parker had the Eleventh, Forty-first, and Fifty-first divisions and the Fifty-seventh Infantry Regiment, all comprising the Second Philippine Corps. MacArthur also had a reserve and service troops—altogether, a strength of about 83,000 men, both Americans and Filipinos.

On the Japanese side, the assault was led by the Sixty-fifth Infantry Brigade under Lieutenant General Akira Nara. Actually these Japanese troops were just out of basic training and knew very little about warfare. The organization originally planned for the assault, the Forty-eighth Infantry Division, was on its way to the Indies.

General Honma was confident of achieving victories as easily and swiftly as those he had already enjoyed, so he decided to send his men down both sides of the peninsula, even though his artillery had not arrived. On the west coast the Japanese did not expect to meet any resistance. On the east coast they expected to find only token resistance. But it was here that their artillery was concentrated.

The battle opened on the afternoon of January 9, with a heavy Japanese artillery bombardment, after which the troops started to move toward Calaguiman. They moved swiftly, believing there would be little resistance, but they had miscalculated the position of the American defense. That first afternoon the Americans responded with counterbombardment. Then, on the morning of January 10, the advancing Japanese troops ran into the American Fifty-seventh Infantry, which stood and fought, and the Japanese advance was stopped. The Japanese Ninth Infantry was to move overland and outflank the Americans, but the Japanese found the going through the rugged country very hard and the harassment by American fire very accurate and painful, and the Ninth Infantry was stopped time and again. It did not come up against the main American positions until six days after the battle began.

The Japanese had planned flanking movements, but the countryside and the American defense made it impossible, so General Nara concentrated all his forces in a frontal attack.

By January 13, the Japanese had managed to cross the Calaguiman River, but their hold was tenuous on both sides, and the Americans sent out reinforcements and eliminated most of the enemy there. The Japanese advance was brought to a halt.

General Honma came up to learn what was wrong, and he decided to rearrange the troops and change the nature of the attack. Part of the force was moved around from the east to the west coast to give the Japanese greater strength where the Americans had less. Major General Kaoki Kimura led the operations on the west coast, and with an additional 5,000 men, he attacked the town of Moron and captured it against only spotty American defenses. This was the first Japanese victory of the campaign.

On January 18 the Japanese advance hit the main line of American resistance for the first time. In five days of hard fighting the Japanese gained ground and broke through that main line of resistance in the area of the American Fifty-first Infantry Division. The U.S. Fifty-first Infantry Regiment was sent to counterattack and did so, gaining back the ground, but at a terrible cost. The Fifty-first Regiment was badly hurt and in no condition to resist the next Japanese attack that came almost immediately. Under attack by two Japanese regiments and worn down by casualties, the Fifty-first Regiment collapsed, giving the Japanese a break 1,000 yards wide in the main line of resistance.

Then the battle settled down to a slogging match. The Japanese, who had not expected such strong resistance, were tiring under the strain. The Americans were also tiring.

But if the Americans were to maintain their line of resistance they had to eliminate the 1,000-yard breakthrough; this meant a counterattack. For three days the Thirty-first Infantry and Forty-fifth Infantry tried, but their attacks were uncoordinated, and by January 19 it was apparent they were not going to be able to seal the break. By January 22 it was clear that the American defense line could not be held.

Late on the afternoon of January 22, General MacArthur came up to the front, examined the situation, and ordered a withdrawal to the rear battle position. The Japanese tried to outflank the Americans in an attack using landing craft, but the landing craft got blown about and the attempt failed. The Japanese found themselves landed in isolated positions, with Americans all around them. The Americans soon located them and, in a series of small actions, annihilated whole pockets of Japanese in what became known as the Battle of the Points. The Japanese attempt to infiltrate and turn the American flank had failed by February 13. The Japanese had sent two infantry battalions to land at Longoskayan, Quinauan, Salaiim, and Anyasan points, and all but 34 of these men had either been killed by the Americans or committed suicide to avoid capture. This was the point at which General Honma had to admit that his attempt to take Bataan quickly had failed.

The battle then became a struggle of attrition. The Japanese were reduced in numbers, with many men sick with malaria and dysentery. But so were the Americans and Filipinos. Both sides were short of food, and the Americans were short of field pieces.

The American rear defense position was shorter and stronger than their main line of resistance had been, but the problem was that if it was breached, there was no place to go.

All this time, from Christmas onward, the American navy presence also remained in the Philippines. Admiral Rockwell, who had been left by Admiral Hart to fight the rearguard action for the navy, had three river gunboats from China, two tugboats, three minesweepers, two civilian tugboats, two converted yachts, two submarine tenders, and six PT boats.

In January the task of the American naval forces was to protect the rear of the army on Bataan and prevent the Japanese from making amphibious landings behind the American lines. When the Americans retreated to the line that runs from Bagac to Orion across Bataan, the navy was there supporting them. During the Japanese attempt to land behind the American lines, the American navy small boats had worked along the shore, using motor launches that were made into "Mickey Mouse battleships" with boiler plate for armor. Each had mounted a light field gun and several machine guns. The American boats went along the shore, shooting up the caves that held the trapped Japanese.

The Japanese tried another landing in an attempt to outflank the Americans on the southwest point of Bataan. The Americans managed to put half a dozen P–40 fighters into the air and also used several of the motor torpedo boats. The army planes sank five barges loaded with Japanese troops, and the PT boats sank three more.

Attrition. That was the sort of war it was. On February 15 the U.S. command put out a communique:

"Fighting in Bataan was limited to local unimportant patrol skirmishes. Forces of the enemy are evidently being regrouped for resumption of the offensive. Japanese units on the front lines are being relieved by fresh troops."

In Tokyo, Imperial General Headquarters had changed its position. Earlier it had not seemed important if the Americans lasted a little longer in the Philippines, because affairs were going so well everywhere else. But now the Japanese in the Philippines were beginning to look like losers, not winners. They were taking very heavy casualties on Bataan, and as far as Imperial Headquarters was concerned, the Fourteenth Army operations had to be considered a failure. The Japanese army called for more bombers to return to the Philippines, and some were brought from as far away as Burma. General Honma was informed that his efforts were less than satisfactory, and by orders of Imperial Headquarters his staff was shaken up. Lieutenant Colonel Tsuji, fresh from the fighting in Singapore, was transferred with a regiment of the Fifth Division to the Philippines, to help put some starch into the Honma campaign.

Among the Americans, malaria, hunger, fear, and fatigue were taking their toll every day. One sergeant recalled the feeling:

"Rumors were rampant. One we all believed was that two shiploads of [American] troops had already landed at

Manila and they were on their way to get us out. We were going to be evacuated, and since we had fought the war, we were to be returned immediately to the States. We believed this. We had nothing to counter these stories and we were very naive. This was the day when soldiers did what they were told and never questioned a senior noncom or officer. We had no radio. We had no telephones. I think the rumors were good, though. It gave us something to believe in. When morale is so bad and there's nothing more to do, rumors help. . . ."

The rumors continued. There was supposed to be a paratroop drop to save the American troops. A convoy was coming in, they said, on Monday, then on Tuesday, and then on Wednesday . . . There was even a sort of psychological buck-up campaign. Someone put out a pamphlet announcing that reinforcements were on the way.

But of course there would be no reinforcements. That decision had been made at the highest level and approved throughout the military establishment. There was no way the American army or navy could put together a relief force sufficiently powerful to retake the Philippines and bring that force to Manila Bay. The idea was not even seriously considered in Washington. Indeed, the new war plan called for the abandonment and later reconquest of the Philippines.

EIGHT

The Fall of Singapore

January 18, 1942.

The Japanese Fifth Division and the Imperial Guards, or most of them, were driving down the road toward the Muar River, with the bicycle troops pedaling as quickly as their bandy legs would move. The Australian and Indian troops knew they were coming; they felled big trees and hauled the logs across the road to make roadblocks. General Yamashita dispatched an entire brigade of the Imperial Guards to land behind the Australian lines.

The main Japanese force reached the banks of the Muar and stopped. The collapsible motorboats were brought up again, and in the middle of the night the Japanese began to cross the river. By daybreak they had established a roadblock in strength. In the light of morning the activity on the bank increased, and more motorboats and sampans hauled Japanese troops across the 600-yard-wide river. They came under fire from Australian 25-pounders, and many of the boats were sunk, with many Japanese killed or drowned. But the Japanese kept coming. The roadblock was pushed back almost to the water's edge and the advantage nearly lost, but more Japanese troops surged up the bank and they held. Slowly they drove the Australians back, although at enormous cost.

The battle proceeded. For 48 hours the Australians gave ground slowly, bitterly, and it seemed they might rally and push the Japanese into the river. The Indians gained heart and together the Allied troops forced the Japanese back.

But at dawn on the third day of battle, a landing party of the Imperial Guards Division appeared at the Australian rear and cut them off from supplies and reinforcements. Japanese troops set up roadblocks. The only way out for the Australians and Indians was to force the Japanese back or to jump into the swampy jungle on either side of the road. The Japanese, reinforced from across the river, gained strength. The Australians, without supplies, lost ground quickly. Soon most of their battalion commanders and other officers were dead. The survivors of the 4,500-man force went into the jungle and made their way in small groups toward the British lines. But in the end only 850 of the Australians and Indians made it. They had held Yamashita up for almost a week.

The Imperial Guards Division was furious at being out-fought by the enemy, and General Nishimura led them in one of the worst atrocities of the war. They beheaded 200 wounded men and were seen doing so by survivors who were hiding in the jungle.

During the battle, the commander of the Third Regiment of the Guards had been wounded. Usually it was the pre-rogative of the division commander to choose his regimental commanders, but in this case, Yamashita showed his dis-approval of the Imperial Guards Division's behavior by sending to Tokyo for a new commander. General Nishimura was furious and became more uncooperative than ever with Yamashita. The Imperial Guards outdid themselves in brav-ery, audacity, and ferocity. Even dying soldiers roused themselves for one more shot at the enemy before they gasped their lives away. The Australians and the Indians also fought fiercely. They charged the Japanese lines time and time again. Brigadier Duncan, commander of the Forty-fifth Indian Brigade, himself led a charge into the Japanese line, brandishing his saber, and was shot down and killed.

As the battle on the Muar River was raging, Yamashita also moved the Eighteenth Division down the other side of the Malay Peninsula. They went down the swampy Endau River estuary, 100 miles north of Johore Strait. They were thrown back by the defenders at first, but the next day a convoy of two troop ships, two cruisers, and 12 destroyers landed troops at the estuary. This was the main Japanese attack force that would move against Singapore.

The British rushed a pair of destroyers up to challenge the Japanese convoy, and they sank one Japanese destroyer, but one British destroyer was also sunk.

The British tried to stop the Japanese with their air power. They had just received 50 Hurricane fighter planes from Britain, and these were thrown into the battle. So were Buffalo fighters, Hudson bombers, and Wildebeest and Albacore bombers. But the Japanese naval air fighters, based now on airfields in Malaya, came up to meet the British attack, and the Zeros completely outmatched the British planes. The Hurricanes came crashing down. The Japanese lost 13 Zeros in the fight, but the British lost all their air power; after this battle they could no longer launch an air strike.

The Australians prepared an ambush, and the Japanese walked into it and lost 300 men. But this was the last big fight on the Malay peninsula. General Wavell in Java gave the British in Malaya permission to withdraw into Singapore fortress, and on the night of January 31 they did. At 8:15 on the morning of February 1, the rear guard, the Argyll and Sutherland Highlanders, pipes skirling, marched across the causeway to Singapore Island, and the causeway was blown up behind them. A 75-foot gap now separated the two sides.

Seven hours later, General Yamashita's advance guard reached the bank of the Johore Strait and the causeway and then moved back to the big rubber plantation there. Yamashita also noted the arrival of the Imperial Guards Division and the Fifth Division. He was making his plans for the attack on Singapore.

He reported to Tokyo:

"We have advanced 1,000 kilometers. We have captured 330 guns, 400 heavy machine guns, 4,000 rifles, 280 armored cars and other vehicles, and [have] rebuilt 250 bridges. We have captured 8,000 prisoners and estimate the enemy dead to be 5,000."

General Yamashita moved into the big bungalow on the rubber plantation at Johore and spent four days planning his attack, which would send the Fifth and Eighteenth divisions across the causeway. The Imperial Guards would remain in reserve.

General Nishimura was extremely annoyed to learn that his Imperial Guards would not lead the attack on Singapore and he went into a sulk. That was one of Yamashita's problems. A more serious problem was the shortage of ammunition. The Japanese soldiers now had only a hundred rounds of ammunition each. General Yamashita was short of rice, and even though his men could subsist on two bowls of rice a day, they were not going to get even that if the campaign lasted very long. He had only 30,000 men and 18 tanks left.

As for the British, they had 100,000 troops in Singapore, but that number was deceptive in terms of strength; many of the Indian and the Australian troops were hardly trained at all.

In the first week of February each side scouted the other— the enemy. Each did so by sending patrols to swim in the strait. Using information gathered this way, the British reported that large Japanese forces were lurking in the rubber plantation across the way.

The Japanese began bombing and shelling Singapore, and General Percival, the defending commander, got the impression that they had brought up more guns and ammunition. But that was a bluff on Yamashita's part. He was expending bits of his precious ammunition supply to convince the British of just that. Yamashita then moved his headquarters into the palace of the sultan of Johore, on top of the hill overlooking the strait. There he was only a mile away from his enemies and within range of their artillery and small arms.

On February 8 the British set fire to the Singapore oil tanks, and that night the sky was lit up with the flames. Yamashita feared that they would set fire to the oil that was seeping into the strait, thus preventing the Japanese from crossing. But for some reason the British did not think of this obvious move.

Yamashita's supply officer, Colonel Ikatini, came to him to ask that the general call off the attack and wait for supplies to come from Japan. The colonel did not think he could feed the troops for even a week longer, and he feared that the attack would fail because they would run out of ammunition and gasoline. But Yamashita had an even greater concern. He feared that the British would soon receive reinforcements from Australia or India and that they would then break out of Singapore, attack his troops with their now greater force, and drive the Japanese back up the Malay Peninsula.

Yamashita realized he could not wait; he knew the supply system was so confused it would be weeks before he could expect reinforcements, ammunition, and food. So he had to attack, even though his force was only a third the size of the enemy and his supplies were almost exhausted.

Just before midnight, the Japanese Fifth Division began the attack. By midnight they had cut the Australian telephone wires and had split the two Australian battalions that defended the strait. The Australians retreated, and the Japanese Fifth Division was soon ashore on Singapore Island, followed shortly by the Eighteenth Division. The Australians panicked and broke ranks. Yamashita was afraid the British would launch a powerful counterattack and overwhelm his small force that was now ashore in Singapore. But the British believed that Yamashita had more than a hundred thousand men standing by, and General Percival failed to act.

Yamashita was having trouble with the Imperial Guards Division. They had been ordered to cross into the swamp at the mouth of the Kranji River, but General Nishimura, without informing Yamashita, decided not to attack. This might have meant disaster for the Japanese, but since the British didn't take advantage of this failure, just 24 hours after the attack began, Yamashita was able to move headquarters across the strait and onto Singapore Island itself.

Nishimura still had not attacked and did not until Yamashita issued a direct order telling him to do so. By that time the British had finally thought to set fire to the oily waters of the strait. As a result of Nishimura's delay, many of his Imperial Guards were either burned to death or lost in the rising tide.

Japanese engineering troops were now repairing the broken causeway, and the day after the attack began it was again usable for transport. Soon Japanese tanks were moving into Singapore. By afternoon the Japanese had reached the edge of the Tengah airport, where they came under the fire of the British 40-centimeter guns.

General Wavell came up from Java to consult with General Percival. What he saw was a force in virtual panic. One battalion of the Forty-fourth Indian Brigade had been given permission to withdraw from a difficult position. Seeing this, the rest of the brigade also retreated, and the retreat soon became a disorderly flight.

Yamashita's tanks moved forward and attacked down the Bukit Timah road. On February 11, Yamashita called on the British to surrender Singapore even as his ammunition was running out. Yamashita moved his headquarters into a wrecked factory near Bukit Timah. The British shortened their line and dug in. Yamashita feared they would do just that and that reinforcements would reach them. He surrounded the city as completely as he could. He needed the Imperial Guards to close the ring, but General Nishimura again refused to obey orders. He complied only when Yamashita sent his deputy chief of staff to the guards with a written order to move into position near the water reservoir.

General Gordon Bennett, the commander of the Australians, told the Australian prime minister by radio that he was going to surrender to prevent further loss of life, and then he personally managed to escape from Singapore.

The Imperial Guards, closing in on the reservoir, were thrown back by the Second Indian Brigade, which fought very hard. But Singapore was a shambles; there was fighting in the streets, shops and offices were deserted and damaged by shelling, and corpses had been left blackening and stinking in the sun. The word was passed to General Percival that the potable water supply would last only another 24 hours, and there were a million people in the city, including many thousands of refugees who had fled to Singapore from northern Malaya.

The Japanese troops rushed through the streets, bayoneting civilians, raping, and rioting. They broke into the military hospital at Alexandra and there claimed that someone had fired on them, so they murdered 150 patients and staff members, including a patient lying on an operating table.

General Percival asked General Wavell for permission to surrender.

On February 14 General Percival decided to surrender. The next day, Captain Sugita, leader of a company of the Fifth Division, which was a mile from Bukit Timah, saw three British officers waving a white flag. They approached while his troops held their fire. Sugita sent a message to General Yamashita, and the general replied telling the captain to accept the surrender and inform the British that Yamashita would meet them at 6 P.M. at the Ford automobile factory at Bukit Timah. Yamashita arrived first with five staff officers. They sat on one side of a long table covered with a white cloth. Percival arrived late with his staff and sat on the other side.

Yamashita was very nervous because he suddenly realized that the British had 100,000 troops instead of the 40,000 he had estimated. He wanted to get the surrender over with quickly, and his manner with Percival was very brusque. He demanded immediate and total surrender with no conditions. Percival tried to negotiate.

"I want to hear nothing from him except yes or no," Yamashita told his interpreter.

The next day Captain Sugita, who had accepted that first British overture of surrender, led a victory march through a burning Singapore, to the palace of the British governor, where he hoisted the flag of the Rising Sun.

Yamashita then had to deal with the disposal of 100,000 prisoners of war. General Nishimura was no help. Yamashita finally tired of the general's attitude and reported it to Count Terauchi at Saigon. As a result the Imperial Guards Division did not receive the thanks from the Emperor that the men expected, and the division was disgraced. Nishimura went back to Japan where he was relieved of command. His chief of staff, General Imaye, was demoted and sent to Manchukuo as a regimental commander.

Friends were supporting Yamashita for the job of war minister, but General Tojo hated Yamashita (whom he knew to be much more able than himself), and so he prevented Yamashita's promotion. He even stopped Yamashita from paying a call on Emperor Hirohito, which a victorious field commander had the right to do. Tojo transferred Yamashita immediately after the fall of Singapore to Manchukuo and the Kwantung Army, where he was put in charge of the First Army group. Theoretically this was a very important job, or would have been had the Japanese retained their intention of attacking Russia. But Tojo had realized after the Nomonhon disaster of 1940 that Japan could not successfully attack the USSR, and so the great Kwantung Army that had been built up was actually useless, and Yamashita was "in Siberia," for all practical purposes. Thus did Prime Minister Tojo deal with his enemy, the man who had carried out one of the most remarkable military campaigns in the history of modern warfare. Ignored by the emperor, the prime minister, and the Imperial General Headquarters, Yamashita would still go down in history as "the Tiger of Malaya," and his defeat of a force three times larger than his own would be seen as the major Japanese army victory in the early days of the Pacific War.

NINE

Striking the Indies

In December 1941 the Japanese naval air forces were moving more rapidly than the Allies could imagine—by sea, but not with ships; airplanes were the reason. New naval air bases were established wherever the Japanese army took control.

From Eleventh Air Fleet headquarters at Tainan on Taiwan came orders to establish forward airfields in the Sulu Islands, halfway between Mindanao and Borneo, 1,200 miles from Tainan. On December 30, 27 fighter planes were ordered to move up as the advance echelon. Once they arrived at Jolo, they were immediately moved again—so great was the need for fighter protection. They flew another 270 miles south to Tarakan on the east coast of Borneo. From there they began to give air protection to Japanese convoys moving into the East Indies.

In January 1942 the Allies prepared for their last-ditch stand in the Far East, the defense of Java, with a combined command headed by British Field Marshal Sir Archibald Wavell, who had just been promoted. Lieutenant General Brett of the United States was the air commander and deputy commander of the whole, and British General Sir H. R. Pownall was chief of staff. Admiral Hart became overall naval commander, at the same time the Asiatic Fleet was dissolved, and Admiral Glassford was promoted and given the job of commander of U.S. Naval Forces in the southwest Pacific. Admiral Hart spent his time at Marshal Wavell's headquarters, and Admiral Glassford ran the fleet from Surabaya. The service base for the fleet was at Darwin, Australia 1,200 miles away, much too far for comfort.

The Japanese were moving fast. They occupied northern Sarawak in mid-December. Then they took Brunei Bay and also entered the Celebes Sea, with landings at Jesselton and the Menado Peninsula and Tarakan Island.

The Americans sent B–17 bombers, which did considerable damage to the Tarakan installations, but the Japanese controlled the northern approaches to the Makassar Strait.

Several American submarines began operations out of Surabaya, but the Japanese had the bases on both coasts of northern Borneo. The next important task for the Japanese was the capture of Balikpapan, which began on January 21, 1942, when 16 Japanese transports put out from Tarakan with an escort of patrol boats. The task force was attacked by American submarines and planes, and one transport, the *Nana Maru,* was set afire. But that night Japanese minesweepers entered the area along the Borneo coast, and a few hours later their transports anchored, protected by a cruiser and a dozen destroyers.

Admiral Glassford's task force was then anchored at Kupang Bay at the Dutch end of Timor Island. He learned of the Japanese movements on the morning of January 20. He took the cruisers *Marblehead* and *Boise* and four destroyers to attack. But the American ships were not in good shape. The *Marblehead* was running without one of her turbines, while the *Boise* grounded on an uncharted rock during this venture and was badly damaged. So Glassford sent the cruisers back to Warroda Bay, where he switched his flag from the *Boise* to the *Marblehead* and then set off again to look for action, while the *Boise* went down the coast of Java to find a Dutch base and have her damaged bottom inspected.

The forces were building fast for a battle.

The Japanese Second Fleet had overall supervision of

southwest Pacific operations. Its commander was Vice Admiral Nobutake Kondo. Admiral Takahashi commanded the Third Fleet, which covered the Philippines, and Vice Admiral Ozawa commanded the Southern Expeditionary Force, which was moving into the East Indies.

The Americans, British, and Dutch had among them two cruisers, five light cruisers, and 22 destroyers, as well as a number of PBY scout bombers, various support ships, and 40 submarines.

The Japanese had two battleships, seven aircraft carriers, 13 cruisers, six light cruisers, more than 50 destroyers, dozens of submarines, plus scores of support craft and a whole system of naval air bases that they had built in the islands as they captured them.

As the Japanese moved toward Balikpapan, it was apparent that the *Marblehead* was in no condition to fight, so she was moved south of Balikpapan, where Admiral Glassford could, theoretically at least, direct the battle.

The real responsibility for the Americans was placed in the hands of Commander Paul Talbot of Destroyer Division 59. He had four destroyers, the *John D. Ford,* the *Pope,* the *Parrott,* and the *Paul Jones.* They were all old four-stack destroyers that burned coal, hardly a match for the brand-new destroyers of the Japanese fleet but the best the Americans had in the area.

On the afternoon of January 23, the *Ford* led the other three ships in a column up along the coast of Celebes Island. They were steaming at 20 knots, which was pretty close to maximum, considering their boilers. Commander Talbot was going in to attack the Japanese invasion fleet at Balikpapan, first with torpedoes and then with gunfire.

The commander was eager to avoid contact with snooping planes, and he was lucky. They saw no enemy planes, only a single PBY patrol bomber. As the ships moved up the coast, the radio reported that Dutch bombers had attacked Japanese ships at Balikpapan and had destroyed several of them. So the enemy was already there. Also, the Dutch had set fire to the refineries so the American destroyers would have targets and the light of the fires to shoot by.

After sunset the destroyers reached Cape Mandar and turned toward Balikpapan. Orders were issued for a night torpedo attack, and ship speed was moved up to 26 knots, which, for those ships, was almost a miraculous feat. They headed in straight for Balikpapan lightship; then at 8 P.M. Talbot called for everything they could get in the way of speed and they managed to raise it to 27 knots!

Four hours passed, the stokers sweating with a will in the fire rooms. The ships' lookouts saw fires ahead, and the Americans knew they were coming to Balikpapan. At 2 A.M. the column took an oblique approach to the line of Japanese transport ships they could see anchored in a neat row about five miles outside the harbor.

Then out of the blackness came a flashing blue light, and a Japanese armored cruiser loomed ahead. Commander Talbot ordered a change of course and headed for the Japanese ship, still at 27 knots. The ships passed each other so swiftly, both moving at high speed, that the Japanese thought they were seeing Japanese destroyers. A division of Japanese destroyers also passed the American ships but paid them no attention.

The American ships moved into the harbor. The torpedo tubes had long since been trained outward. The tension was unbearable for the captain of the *Parrott*, who launched prematurely; all its torpedoes missed their targets. The destroyer veered to port and fired another spread at another target, but once again there were no explosions. This failure may have been partly the fault of the skipper and the torpedo officer, but part most certainly was the fault of the torpedoes. The Americans had not yet begun to learn that their torpedoes tended to be defective.

The captain of the *Ford*, more conservative, fired one torpedo at the minesweeper, but she was moving fast and the torpedo missed. The *Paul Jones* also fired one torpedo and also missed.

Captain Talbot now took his flotilla south to come in for another attack. The *Parrott* was traveling parallel to the anchored transport ships and a burning tanker, and she fired another spread of three torpedoes from her port tubes. Suddenly the Americans were gratified by the sight and sounds of a tremendous explosion as one of the ships blew up. She was obviously carrying explosives; the debris went high. She sank immediately with all hands.

The Japanese now knew they were under attack. Rear Admiral Nishimura was on the light cruiser *Naka* and had with him nine destroyers and several minesweepers and a subchaser. He went out into the strait looking for submarines, thus missing a chance to confound the American attack. There was a reason for his action; a few hours earlier a Dutch submarine had sunk the Japanese transport *Jukka Maru*, so the admiral was correct in supposing that submarines were a danger.

Commander Talbot ordered his captains to move in, and Lieutenant Commander W. C. Blinn in the *Pope* rushed in and fired a spread of five torpedoes. The other three destroyers also fired several torpedoes. One struck the freighter *Tatsukami Maru* and it blew up and sank—probably it, too, was carrying explosives or high-test gasoline.

The American destroyers were getting low on torpedoes at this point. Commander Talbot led them back again toward the Japanese ships at anchor, saw what he thought was a destroyer, and torpedoed it. It was actually a small torpedo boat. At the same time *Pope* and *Parrott* also fired at the vessel; altogether this 750-ton ship was hit by three torpedoes and was literally blown out of water by an excess of explosives.

By this time the Japanese had the wind up; the transports began hauling up anchor and getting under way. Searchlights and the flames of burning ships lit up the harbor. The American ships kept maneuvering, firing more torpedoes. The *Ford* put a torpedo into a Japanese transport just as she turned from her anchorage. She was the *Kureatake Maru*, another munitions ship, and she blew up with a very satisfying roar.

Now the American destroyers became separated. The

Ford turned toward the line of Japanese ships and the *Pope* did too, but lost her leader in the lights. The *Parrott,* which was out of torpedoes, retired. The *Paul Jones* followed her out. The *Pope* was also out of torpedoes, but she had her guns, and she began firing at the merchant ships with the four-incher. One small shell hit the *Pope,* damaging her and wounding four men. Another fragment hit a gasoline tank below and started a fire. Meanwhile the *Ford* kept firing at the Japanese, putting the enemy battery on one ship out of action. Commander Talbot had one more torpedo. He turned in toward the shore, and in the light from the burning ships saw another large transport to port. He gave the order to fire, and the torpedo officer fired that last torpedo. It exploded against the transport, which then began to burn. That was the last the men of the *Ford* saw of the ship as they moved away at top speed.

The American destroyers headed away from Balikpapan to rendezvous with the flagship *Marblehead.* At dawn the four destroyers met the *Marblehead.* All of them were relatively sound. They had run through the Japanese fleet in the first real American naval assault action of the Pacific war, and they had comported themselves well, especially considering the faulty state of many of their torpedoes. They had sunk three of twelve transports as well as a patrol craft and had damaged several other ships, one of which was definitely torpedoed, although not sunk.

The Americans had achieved a naval victory, which improved their relations with the Dutch and the British, who had been very critical of the American defeat at Pearl Harbor. But their victory did nothing to improve relations between Admiral Hart and Admiral Glassford. Hart felt that Glassford was somehow responsible for everything that had gone wrong—the grounding of the *Boise,* the bad boilers of the *Marblehead,* and the difficulties of the destroyer *Peary* in the past. Hart was also angry that he had been deposed as commander of the Asiatic Fleet and that Glassford had been given tactical command of American fighting ships in the East Indies.

Glassford, for his part, was furious because Admiral Hart had gone over his head and issued orders directly to Commander Talbot to make the destroyer torpedo attack when Glassford's flagship was out of action. He wrote in his diary that things had gotten to the point where either he or Admiral Hart would have to leave the area. Glassford was particularly angry because he had coached Commander Talbot in the tactics the destroyers had used in the attack, basing his instructions on information he had received about a British torpedo attack delivered under similar circumstances in World War I, and he felt the victory was as much his as it was that of the men who had fought so bravely in the action. To have Hart try to take it away from him was infuriating.

Back in Washington Admiral King showed that he agreed with Admiral Glassford. He had earlier indicated that Admiral Hart should give up his operational command when he took over on the Wavell staff, and Hart had ignored that hint. Now Admiral King issued a direct order to Hart to stop interfering.

Admiral Glassford pulled into Surabaya with the fleet on January 25 and went to navy headquarters. There he learned to his delight what Admiral King was saying, and with a happy heart went to the Orangjie Hotel to celebrate. That night he gave a party for the staff at the Simpang Club. The next day Admiral Hart came down from Bandoeng to attend several meetings. He could hardly control his fury at Glassford and King for having issued the order. The two of them managed to put on a brave face with the Dutch and the British, and then Glassford went back down to Surabaya. On January 31 official word came of Admiral Glassford's advancement from rear admiral to vice admiral, and that night he gave another party.

Admiral Hart stayed up in Bandoeng and nursed his grudges. Whether the defense of the Dutch East Indies would have been helped if the two American admirals had been friends instead of enemies is debatable, but certainly their open enmity did the situation little good.

TEN

The Juggernaut Advances

Although the battle of Balikpapan was an American victory, it made not the slightest difference in the course of events in the Pacific in this period; it failed to slow the Japanese juggernaut even slightly.

By the end of January, the Japanese forces were firmly entrenched on both sides of the South China Sea, in the Makassar Strait, and on the Molucca Sea. They were also rapidly converging on Java and Sumatra.

The Japanese had the great advantage of a unified naval command, while, because the Americans, British, and Dutch formed an alliance of three nations, by its very nature theirs was a divided command, held together at the top by the Wavell organization but with each nation's defense forces working in separate areas rather than together. Perhaps it was impossible for them to work closely together. It took years for the postwar North Atlantic Treaty Organization forces to bring together the fighting forces of the Western powers; it was too much to expect the new, hastily flung-together ABDA—American, British, Dutch, Australia—organization to function smoothly. Each nation's forces tended to look out for itself and often forgot to inform the other allies of developments in time for them to be of any assistance.

On the afternoon of January 23, an American PBY sighted a large enemy surface force moving toward Balikpapan and alerted a force of B–17s to attack. They did some damage but not enough to stop the Japanese force, which was moving on Kendari in southeastern Celebes.

At 5:30 on the morning of January 24 the American seaplane tender *Childs* was moving out of Kendari Bay when enemy vessels were sighted. The *Childs* might have been a goner, but suddenly a storm cloud appeared ahead and the *Childs* steamed into it. Twenty minutes later more Japanese warships appeared, but the *Childs* ran into another convenient storm cloud.

The *Childs* continued to steam on for two hours. Then she was attacked by six Zero fighters but managed to escape without damage. But the Japanese invasion force took Kendari; it now controlled the short route between Java and Australia and was in bombing range of Surabaya.

After taking Kendari the Japanese attacked Ambon, an island 350 miles eastward, using two seaplane carriers and several destroyers. (Japan made more use of seaplane carriers as an attack force than did the Western powers and used them more skillfully.) In the Ambon attack the two seaplane carriers functioned along with the aircraft carriers *Soryu* and *Hiryu*. On January 27 an attack force of transports sailed for Ambon, escorted by the cruisers *Nachi*, *Haguro*, and *Jintsu*, plus about a dozen destroyers. This force was under the command of Rear Admiral Raizo Tanaka, and it was joined by several minesweepers and more escorts.

To defend against this large force, the allies had a handful of old aircraft on Ambon. The Japanese came on January 31 and simply overwhelmed the Allied defenders. The battle lasted three days; at the end of it, all the Dutch and Australian troops who had not been killed were prisoners of war.

On February 3, the Japanese air force made its first raid on Surabaya and destroyed a large number of Dutch aircraft. That meant the Japanese had already put the airfield at Kendari into operation and there would be more of the same.

So Admiral Hart ordered the submarine tenders *Holland* and *Otus* diverted to Tjilatjap on the south coast of Java. The harbor was far from ideal, but it was all the Allies had.

After Balikpapan, Dutch Admiral Doorman took over command of the combined striking force, which now included the American cruiser *Houston* and the destroyers *Paul Jones, Pillsbury,* and *Whipple* as well as the *Marblehead* and its destroyers, the *Stewart, Edwards, Barker,* and *Bulmer*.

Admiral Doorman wanted to hit the Japanese in Makassar Strait, where Allied observation planes had spotted a Japanese naval force. So in the Dutch light cruiser *De Ruyter* he led the force out of Bunda Roads just after midnight of February 4. The *De Ruyter* was in the lead, with the *Houston,* the *Marblehead,* and the Dutch cruiser *Tromp* all in a line behind her. Four American destroyers were on the flanks of the formation, with four Dutch destroyers in the rear.

In the morning, Admiral Doorman learned that nearly 40 Japanese planes were on their way to hit Surabaya: twin-engined bombers of the Eleventh Air Fleet. They were indeed based at Kendari, as everyone had suspected.

At 9:49 that morning the men on the bridge of the *Marblehead* saw four formations of nine bombers each, traveling at 17,000 feet altitude. The *Marblehead* went to general quarters. The cruiser started up all her boilers and got ready for a fight.

Six minutes later the Japanese began their attack. The *Marblehead* had moved away from the other ships to gain "fighting room"—that was the philosophy of the time, before the American fleet learned to bunch up its ships and rely on mutual antiaircraft defenses with about double the number of guns of the ships of 1941.

Captain Robinson of the *Marblehead* watched the planes as they came down to 14,000 feet above the ship. When he believed they were about ready to bomb he ordered full left rudder and increased speed. But the Japanese did not bomb. They circled around and came back for another pass. Again the captain guessed and swerved, and again the Japanese did not bomb. On the third pass they bombed, dropping a stick of seven bombs about 100 yards off the port bow. They did no damage, and the ship's gunners shot down one bomber.

Another Japanese plane was hit, and the pilot tried to crash the *Marblehead*. The 50-caliber machine guns were concentrated on the plane as it came in, and it swerved off and crashed in the sea. But at about 10:30 seven bombers came in and straddled the *Marblehead* with high explosive bombs. One bomb hit squarely, pierced the deck, and exploded below, wiping out the sick bay and wrecking the wardroom. Fires broke out. A near miss started more fires. A third bomb landed on the fantail, destroyed the after living quarters, and wrecked the hand steering. The rudder jammed hard left, and fires broke out. The cruiser began going in circles. Captain Robinson speeded to 25 knots, and the ship moved around swiftly in concentric circles.

The damage-control parties started to fix the rudder even as the Japanese planes continued to attack. But the plane did not hit the *Marblehead* at that time. They concentrated their fire on the *De Ruyter* and damaged her. Other planes went after the *Houston* and dropped one big bomb on her deck, killing 50 men and knocking out the after gun turret. The shrapnel from the bomb seemed to be everywhere. The *Houston* then headed for Bali Strait and managed to find a squall to hide in. Then she ran from squall to squall and was not attacked again. The *Marblehead* was still steaming in circles, but by noon the repair parties had done enough to let her follow a crooked course by using her engines for steering, and she headed for Lombok Strait. The *DeRuyter* and the destroyers followed along with *Marblehead* until late that night when the captain said his ship could look after herself, and then Admiral Doorman took the escort on ahead.

The admiral then continued along the southern coast of Java and moved to Batavia. Admiral Hart, who was in overall command of naval forces, was very angry with the

Dutch admiral for retiring, and he ordered Doorman to meet him at Tjilatjap.

They met on February 8, and while they were meeting they got word that the Japanese were moving around the southern tip of Celebes. Hart ordered Doorman to make an attack.

Admiral Hart then inspected the *Marblehead* and the *Houston*. The *Houston*'s after turret was knocked out, but so great was the admiral's need that he decided to keep her in service anyhow, since he had nothing much else to offer. The *Marblehead* was in such terrible shape that the Dutch repair crew wondered whether she could even make her way home. The Dutch did not have the drydock facilities to repair her rudder, so she went home on her engines by way of Ceylon, escorted by the tender *Otus*. Somehow the skipper managed to get her home in one piece.

Those Japanese who had worried Admiral Hart were actually on their way to Makassar Town, where they landed and marched overland to Banjermassin. Other Japanese troops landed at Makassar, and so that was the end of that base. During that operation the American submarine *S–37*, operating out of Surabaya, managed to torpedo and sink the Japanese destroyer *Natsushio*, but that was the Allies' only success there.

By February 10 the Japanese were closing in on the Allied naval forces in the Indies. With the fall of Singapore, the Japanese naval and army forces in that area could all be diverted to Java and were.

As Admiral Hart could see, the Japanese were also ringing Java with air bases and would soon be able to attack anywhere at will.

There was one small consolation: the American tenders came up from Darwin and at last at Tjilatjap the American warships were able to get the repairs they needed so badly. The port was jammed with ships, for it was the only port in the area outside the Japanese bombing range. But for how long? The Japanese were steadily closing in on Java.

ELEVEN

Invading Java

They called it the Japanese Octopus, the huge mass of ships, planes, and military units that was descending on the Dutch East Indies from two sides, through the Makassar Strait and the Molucca Sea and through the South China Sea via the Karimata Strait, and heading for southern Sumatra. The Japanese knew precisely where they were going and how they were going to get there, and as the days wore on, their drive became ever more juggernaut-like. The fall of Singapore freed ships, planes, and men to fight in the Indies. Most of the Philippines fell, and that released even more men, ships, and planes.

On February 6, six transports carrying the Sasebo special landing troops left the new Japanese base at Kendari's Staring Bay, heavily escorted by 15 destroyers and many smaller ships, to land on Makassar and secure that area. The Japanese lost only 10 men in the battle; the only real opposition came from the American submarine *S–37*, which torpedoed the destroyer *Musashio*. There was no other force available to fight. Admiral Doorman considered going out, but he had only two cruisers and two destroyers available for action just then.

The next Japanese action was against Banka Island, which controlled 10 percent of the world tin production, and then

Palembang, the center of the Sumatran oil industry. These two areas were more important to the Japanese than any place they had yet captured.

The Allied naval forces in Java on February 13, 1942, consisted of the Dutch cruisers *De Ruyter*, *Java*, and *Tromp;* the British cruiser *Exeter*; the Australian cruiser *Hobart;* four Dutch destroyers and six American destroyers; and the battered American cruiser *Houston*, her rear turret knocked out. The American cruiser *Marblehead* was out of it, making her way tenuously toward home.

Two Japanese convoys were moving toward Java through the South China Sea, covered by the strongest task force yet seen in the southwest Pacific area. Vice Admiral Ozawa led the defense in the cruiser *Chokai*. He had along with him the carrier *Ryujo;* the cruisers *Kumano*, *Mikuma*, *Suzuya*, *Yura*, and *Mogami;* and six destroyers, all heading down from Camranh Bay in Indochina. Rear Admiral Hashimoto was escorting eight transports with five destroyers, five minesweepers, and two submarine chasers. Fourteen more transports were afloat under the control of Captain Kojima, who had a destroyer screen and, overhead, a heavy escort force of aircraft.

Dutch patrol bombers sighted some of these ships moving through the South China Sea, but bad weather for three days made air reconnaissance impossible and for several days more made it very spotty.

As Singapore collapsed, a number of vessels had sailed for Sumatra and Java, carrying refugees and escaping military personnel. These ships, traveling close together, were unlucky enough to be spotted by Admiral Ozawa's air cover and were then bombed repeatedly and fired upon by the warships until all were sunk. But the slaughter delayed the Japanese and also tipped their hand, so that the Allies knew the convoy was heading for Palembang.

Field Marshal Wavell then ordered Admiral Doorman to take the Combined Strike Force out to contest the passage with the Japanese. Doorman assembled his forces.

The cruiser *Exeter* was brought up from south of the Sunda Strait, and other ships were scattered. But late on February 14 Admiral Doorman had assembled the *Exeter, De Ruyter, Java, Tromp,* and *Hobart;* the destroyers *Banckert, Kortenauer, Van Ghent,* and *Van Nes;* and the American destroyers *Barker, Bulmer, John D. Ford, Parrott, Pope,* and *Stewart.*

As Doorman prepared for battle, the Japanese reached Banka Island. Their next step would be to move up the Moesi River to Palembang.

Admiral Ozawa was already moving to attack. On the morning of February 14 his paratroopers dropped on Palembang's two airfields. The Dutch had seven battalions of troops in Sumatra, but it is a big island, and Airfield Number One, not far from Soengai Gerong, was near the oil installation at Pladjoe, but Airfield Number Two was 60 miles away. The Japanese estimated it would take the Dutch some time to bring assault forces to challenge their paratroops. Admiral Ozawa expected to land his Palembang expeditionary force by February 15 to take over from the paratroops.

Admiral Doorman set out for the most direct approach to Palembang, by the Masin Channel through the straits. But these were treacherous waters, and the destroyer *Van Ghent* struck an uncharted reef off Banka Island. The *Banckert* was sent to pick up survivors and take them back to safety.

Meanwhile, Admiral Ozawa's search planes had sighted the Allied fleet and were preparing for a fight. Ozawa sent the advance force of transports up the Moesi River and the main force of transports back up north of Lingga Island to wait. He then took his warships, which vastly outnumbered and outgunned the Allied fleet, south to fight.

Admiral Ozawa wanted to use his air cover to destroy the unity of the Allied fleet before the engagement, but in this he was unlucky, as the Allies would be many times in the future. At the moment there were no dive bombers or torpedo bombers available to him, only twin-engined level bombers whose pilots had been trained in high-altitude work, mostly in China. They were ordered to attack the Allied force as it came and they did, but it was easy for the Allied ships to maneuver to avoid the bombs as they came down, and no hits were made by the Japanese.

Even so, the Japanese planes scored a victory, for after several such attacks, Admiral Doorman decided to call off the battle. He had no air cover. He was expecting dive bombers and torpedo bombers at any moment, and then he knew he was moving against a much larger and stronger force than his own. The Allied force turned back.

Admiral Ozawa then resumed his mission of bringing the transports to Palembang. Those troops were badly needed because the Japanese were encountering fierce resistance at the airfields. At the end of February 14, the Japanese had been able to capture only Airfield Number One. Soengai Gerong and Airfield Number Two were still in Dutch hands. The Japanese had captured the oil installations at Pladjoe, but the Dutch had counterattacked and driven the Japanese out.

By the morning of February 15, the Dutch had assembled many of their troops in the Airfield Number Two area, and the defeat of the Japanese seemed imminent. The Japanese recognized the danger and dropped another paratroop company on Airfield Number One. Also, the first echelon of transports had moved up the Moesi River and had put troops down in barges and boats; they were now coming up river.

That morning and all day long Allied aircraft from Sumatra attacked the Japanese troops, and Admiral Ozawa found he did not have enough planes available to secure air superiority. But the troops moving up the Moesi made all the difference, and as they neared Palembang, the Dutch made ready to move out. That night of February 15, the Moesi force and the paratroops linked up as the Dutch moved. Two days later the main force arrived, Palembang was securely in Japanese hands, and the troops were sent off toward Sunda Strait in pursuit of the fleeing Allies.

By February 17 most of the Allied personnel had been evacuated across Sunda Strait, leaving huge masses of equipment behind them. A British landing party returned to Oosthaven a day or two later and managed to salvage a lot of aircraft parts, which were badly needed in Java, but Sumatra was lost. It had taken the Japanese only three days to capture the island and its mineral resources.

Now the Japanese moved in the east.

On February 19, the sun came up bright and hot in Darwin, Australia, the major port on the northern coast. It was a summer sun, and it brushed its way through feathery clouds. Just before 8 o'clock that morning Lieutenant Commander E. Grant, commander of the American seaplane tender *William B. Preston,* went ashore to see about delivery of aviation gasoline to keep his little fleet of PBY patrol bombers flying.

Grant's boat had to thread its way among the many ships anchored in Darwin harbor: the Australian hospital ship *Manunda,* the destroyer *Peary,* just back from a mission, Australian troopships and Australian freighters, sloops of war, and a tanker, the *Benjamin Franklin.*

As Grant moved, so did a major Japanese strike force under Vice Admiral N. Kondo: two battleships, three heavy cruisers, and four aircraft carriers commanded by Vice Admiral Chuichi Nagumo. So easy had the Japanese operations in Malaya, the Philippines, and the East Indies been that there was talk in Tokyo about invading Australia. Admiral Kondo's force was coming to hit Darwin and thus soften up the most important port of northern Australia, perhaps to prepare for that invasion.

Nearly 200 aircraft from the four carriers headed toward the city, along with 50 of the twin-engined land-based bombers that had harried Admiral Doorman two days earlier.

At 9:50 that morning the crew of the *Preston* received the air alert, and because their captain had kept his boilers going in anticipation of trouble, the *Preston* was able to move almost immediately and head toward Walker Shoals.

But getting out of the crowded harbor was not easy; it

was somewhat like threading a needle, and the *Preston* moved slowly. She was attacked by bombers that came in at 10:10 and was struck by a 100-pound bomb that knocked out her steering.

The destroyer *Peary* was hit; the bomb must have struck a magazine, for she blew up immediately and sank.

Then six 9-plane formations, level bombers, came in overhead at 10:20 and bombed the town and the docks. The dive bombers came in against the ships. They hit an ammunition ship at the dock, and it blew up. Then they hit another and the fiery performance was repeated. They hit the American transport *Tulagi,* and she went down by the stern. The American transport *Meigs* was on fire, and her men were dropping over the side. Most of the planes avoided the hospital ship with its green stripe and red crosses, but one careless bomber dropped a bomb on her. Fortunately it was a dud.

Three of Skipper Grant's PBYs had been moored in the harbor. They were strafed and began to burn.

From the airfields nearby came P–40 fighters to challenge the Japanese, but they were no match for the Zero fighters, and several were shot down.

Darwin was completely unprepared to meet any sort of air attack. It had no antiaircraft guns around the harbor installations and only a single wharf that would accommodate only two ships at one time.

The town was built mostly of wood, and the buildings blazed up and burned furiously in the attack. The airfield was strafed, and 16 planes were destroyed on the ground and another four in the air as they tried to escape. The wharf and dockyard were wrecked, and the oil and water pipes were broken. Burning oil poured into the water and endangered ships and the men escaping from sinking ships. About 500 Allied personnel were killed in this attack, while the Japanese lost only five planes.

The planes came in waves, returned to their ships, and came again. The attack lasted until 1 o'clock in the afternoon, and when it was over, Darwin was in shambles. Eight ships had been sunk and nine had been damaged. Only two vessels remained undamaged.

As the Japanese naval force was assaulting Darwin and thus wiping out the most important supply port for the Allies in Java, two other Japanese forces were on the move. One invaded Bali and the other landed on the island of Timor. The idea of all three movements was to cut off Java from the east. On Bali the Japanese gained control of the airfield at Den Passar; this would help in their move against Java. It was, after all, only 100 miles from Surabaya. By taking Timor the Japanese broke the fighter air link between Java and Australia.

The Timor invasion force sailed on February 17 from Amboina. Two operations were in the works. First would be the capture of Koepang, the capital of Dutch Timor, and Dili, the capital of Portuguese Timor. Koepang would be first, and the troops meant for that city were carried in nine transports guarded by the cruiser *Jintsu* and eight destroyers. Next day another force of five transports, two destroyers, and several smaller vessels sailed for Dili, on the northeast coast of Timor. Although Portugal was neutral in the war, the Australians and Dutch had troops stationed there; this gave the Japanese the excuse they needed to attack.

The two landings on Timor came on the night of February 19, and on the morning of February 20 the airborne troops from Kendari were dropped behind Koepang. After two days of heavy fighting the Allied troops mostly faded into the jungle to become guerillas. Dili was taken with almost no opposition.

The guerillas from Kendari operated successfully for about six months, but then, when the Japanese sent in a large number of troops to clean them out, the guerillas were taken out by American submarine. By the winter of 1943 they were all gone.

The Bali occupation force sailed from Makassar on the night of February 17. A battalion of the Imperial Forty-eighth Infantry Division, which had first fought on Luzon in the Philippines, was used for this operation. The Allies knew they were coming, and Field Marshal Wavell decided to try to stop them from taking Bali because it was so close to important ABDA bases.

The Japanese force reached Bali on the evening of February 18 and began landing troops the next morning. That day a group of B–17 Flying Fortresses raided the landing and damaged the transport *Sagami Maru*.

That night, Admiral Doorman made the planned attack on the Japanese forces off Bali. He had the cruisers *De Ruyter* and *Java* and the destroyers *Piet Hein, John D. Ford*, and *Pope*. About seven miles separated the first ship from the last as they steamed through Badung Strait. Then came the cruiser *Tromp* and the four American destroyers. Finally, in a third wave, were eight Dutch torpedo boats.

Japanese and Allies sighted one another almost at the same time as the Allies came in, the Japanese half-hidden against the mass of the mountain behind them. The two Japanese destroyers in harbor left their moorings to gain sea room. They crossed in front of the Allied cruisers; the two sides exchanged fire, but there were no hits. The Japanese destroyers then encountered the three Allied destroyers in the rear, and both sides fired torpedoes and guns. The Japanese sank the *Piet Hein*, and the *Ford* and *Pope* retired. The confusion was enormous, and the Japanese destroyers *Asashio* and *Oshio* found themselves shooting at each other.

Then the second Allied force, the four American destroyers and the *Tromp*, entered the strait. The leading American destroyer, the *Stewart*, was badly damaged. Then the destroyers engaged the *Tromp* and damaged her so badly she had to retire to Australia for repairs. The *Oshio* was also damaged. Two more Japanese destroyers, the *Arashio* and *Michishio*, arrived in the thick of the battle. The *Michishio* was hit repeatedly and knocked dead in the water, but the Allied ships retired instead of staying to finish her off, and so she was saved.

The Dutch torpedo boats, the third echelon of the attack

force, came into the strait, but by the time they arrived the action was over and the Japanese destroyers were escorting their transport out of the area to safety.

Thus ended what became known collectively as the Battle of Badung Strait. It was anything but an Allied victory. A large force of Allied ships had managed to damage only one Japanese destroyer, while the Allies lost a destroyer and had a cruiser and an American destroyer badly damaged. More important, from the Allied point of view—they had failed to prevent or dislodge the Japanese landings on Bali.

So by mid-February the Japanese overlooked the Bali and Lombok channels and the Sunda Strait. As of that time the position of the Allies on Java became completely hopeless. Field Marshal Wavell now estimated the life expectancy of his ABDA command as less than two weeks.

TWELVE

The Japanese Move In

By February 15 it had become apparent there was no way the Japanese could be stopped in the Dutch East Indies. It was apparent to the Americans and the British, that is, but not to the Dutch. For even those Dutch citizens who could see the end could not admit it even to themselves. The Indies had been a part of the Dutch empire for 400 years and several generations of Dutch had grown up in this overheated country. So to Admiral Helfrich and the others, sacrificing all this to the Japanese was a completely impossible thought. They insisted on fighting to the end.

The American military presence, however, was already being moved out. That really meant the submarines, because there was precious little else left of the American Asiatic Fleet. The cruisers *Marblehead* and *Boise* were long gone, heading home to seek repairs. The cruiser *Houston* was only half a ship now, and the *Langley,* the first American aircraft carrier, was so old and so decrepit that she was fit only to ferry planes, not to fly them off. The destroyer *Stewart* came back from the Badoeng Strait battle to go into drydock in Surabaya, but in the floating drydock she rolled over to port and suffered more damage, so that she had to be abandoned right there. Because of this series of events the Japanese would inherit this vessel later.

On February 19, Admiral Glassford, tactical commander of American ships in the Far East, sent the freighter *Collingsworth* to Colombo, Ceylon. She carried the last load of tin that the Western Allies would receive from the Indies tin mines until the war's end.

On February 21 Admiral Helfrich cabled the American-British Combined Chiefs of Staff for help. He could hold out in the Indies, he said bravely, if the Western Allies could provide him with ships and guns and planes. General Porten, commander of the Netherlands East Indies Army, said he would fight to the bitter end. But two days later, Field Marshal Wavell cabled Prime Minister Winston Churchill that nothing would help. The Japanese had already broken the defenses of the Malay barrier, and it would be only a matter of days before they captured Java. There was no point in sending any more ships or planes. As for himself, Wavell said, he would remain until the very end if Churchill wished.

Churchill did not wish. On February 19 General Brereton decided to withdraw the American army air force units to India. Then he left for India. General Brett had already gone to Australia. On February 25, Field Marshal Wavell flew to Colombo. That was the end of the ABDA command, and Dutch officers now took charge of all defense operations. All the armed forces left in the Indies were Dutch except for 7,000 British and 500 American troops and a few American and British ships and planes.

The dispersal went quickly now. On February 25 Admiral Purnell, Glassford's chief of staff, flew to Broome, Australia, and set up a new submarine base in the Gulf of Exmouth. The rest of the staff of the American command left for Sydney in two submarines. All that remained of the air forces were a handful of P–40 fighters and a few bombers. Everybody knew, it would not be long before the Japanese came.

Indeed, they were already on their way. The invasion force of Admiral Kurita's western attack group was sailing. It consisted of four heavy cruisers, three light cruisers, a carrier, and a seaplane tender, as well as many auxiliaries and transports. On February 26 they were sighted. Two days earlier Allied planes had spotted Admiral Nishimura's eastern attack group near Bawean. That day an American submarine sighted another convoy off the Kangean Islands.

Admiral Helfrich estimated that the three convoys would reach Java at about daybreak on February 27. He drew together all his fighting ships, taking them off convoy duty in Javanese waters.

On February 25 at dusk Admiral Doorman set out with three cruisers and seven destroyers to find the Japanese, but he was too early and found no ships. He came back to Surabaya to refuel, arriving just in time to find a message from Admiral Helfrich in Bandoeng, telling him of the Japanese movements and demanding that he attack at once and continue to attack until he had defeated the Japanese force.

On the night of February 26 the Combined Strike Force steamed north and west to find the Japanese but did not. At dawn on February 27 they still had not found the Japanese, but just before nine o'clock in the morning Japanese planes found the Allied force. By that time the British cruisers *Exeter* and *Perth* and the destroyers *Electra, Jupiter,* and *Encounter* had joined up. Most of the Japanese planes attacked the destroyer *Jupiter*. But the American cruiser *Houston*, even though she had no rear turret, did have powerful antiaircraft guns and crews that had used them before quite effectively. They kept the Japanese bombardiers off balance, and seven bombs that were dropped toward the *Jupiter* all missed.

But the bombing worried Admiral Doorman; he turned the strike force around and headed toward Surabaya Strait just after 9:30 that morning. When Admiral Helfrich learned of this he sent Admiral Doorman a strongly worded message to go back east and search for the enemy. But Admiral Doorman chose to disobey the order and retire.

The strike force then came into Surabaya, and as it reached the outer entrance, at 1:27 in the afternoon, Doorman received another message from Admiral Helfrich. Patrol planes had sighted three enemy groups of ships. Since the Japanese ships were nearly upon him, Admiral Doorman had to fight.

There was another Allied force not far away, consisting of the Australian cruiser *Hobart*, the light cruisers *Danae* and *Dragon*, and the destroyers *Scout* and *Tenedos*. They had made a sweep earlier, had found no Japanese, and headed toward Tjilatjap. When they passed through Sunda Strait, this force had turned away and headed for Ceylon, which put it completely out of the Java defense zone.

On that afternoon of February 27 Admiral Doorman's force did not reach Surabaya harbor but turned around and headed back toward the enemy, with the *De Ruyter* leading, the *Exeter* next, then the *Houston*, *Perth*, and *Java*. The cruisers were surrounded by destroyers from the British, United States, and Netherlands navies.

There could hardly have been a more poorly organized force to meet a powerful enemy than Admiral Doorman's task force that day. The worst problem was communications. Admiral Doorman's orders had to be transmitted to the American and British ships by an American liaison officer aboard the flagship *De Ruyter*, who translated them and then sent them to the *Houston*, which then sent them to the other English-speaking ships. There was no written plan of operations; there had been no time to put one together. So from the outset the American, British, and Dutch were confused.

Admiral Doorman asked for air cover from the Dutch air force, but there were only a handful of Brewster fighter planes, and the local air commander decided it was more important that they cover a small force of bombers that was going after the Japanese transports. So Doorman got no air cover.

Soon Japanese planes appeared. They were observation planes from the Japanese cruisers *Haguro* and *Nachi*. Then, when the Allied ships were about 30 miles northwest of Surabaya, they spotted a large force of enemy vessels. Doorman called for top speed, 26 knots, from his cruisers, and they outdistanced the destroyers.

But from the beginning the Allied force was in trouble. It did not even have any float planes to spot for the gunners and gather information. The *Java* had no float plane at all, and those of the other ships had been left behind because the admiral had expected a night engagement in which the float planes would have been more nuisance than assistance.

The Japanese float planes from the *Nachi* and *Haguro* appeared up north. But while the Allied ships were trying to pinpoint their locations, suddenly a Japanese cruiser and a number of destroyers also appeared, crossing the Allied formation's bows from starboard to port. Every minute more Japanese masts appeared on the horizon. The battle was about to begin, the battle that would decide the fate of Java.

It was four o'clock in the afternoon when the heavy cruisers *Nachi* and *Haguro* started firing at the Allied cruisers. The first two Allied ships to come under fire were the *Exeter* and the *Houston,* from a range of 11 miles. Then up came the light cruiser *Jintsu,* followed by a number of destroyers. The *Jintsu* opened fire on the British destroyers and immediately straddled the *Electra.* The latter and the destroyer *Jupiter* tried to fire back at the light cruisers, but their 4.7-inch guns could not reach the Japanese, while the larger Japanese guns could reach them easily.

Admiral Doorman then swung his ships to the left to bring as many guns of his cruisers to bear as possible. The *Exeter* and the *Houston* opened fire. The Americans were using blood-red dye in their shells to identify the splashes, and they soon straddled the *Nachi.* In turn the Japanese straddled the *Exeter* and the *De Ruyter.*

Just before 4:30 that afternoon, Admiral Doorman turned his column to the left again, which meant the Japanese and Allied columns were almost parallel to one another, each within the range of the six-inch guns of the other side. The Japanese had the best of it because they had the three spotting planes in the air and the Allies had none. As a result the Japanese shooting soon showed itself to be more accurate than the Allied fire. The Allied ships were almost continually being straddled, and many near misses sent shrapnel flying about the vessels.

Just after 4:30 the *De Ruyter* took an eight-inch shell in its auxiliary engine room. Fortunately, the shell did not explode. Four minutes later Admiral Doorman turned his column to the right, to close the range with the Japanese. Admiral Takagi, commander of the Japanese force, took this opportunity to order a torpedo attack, which meant an attack by cruisers as well as by destroyers, because all Japanese cruisers carried torpedoes.

The *Perth* was completely out of the battle at this time because her guns could not reach the enemy. Despite this, the Japanese torpedo attack failed because the range was still too great. But the Japanese destroyers did make one brilliant move; as they came up to fire, they also laid down a smoke screen that blocked the Allied view of the Japanese cruisers. As a result, using their spotter planes, the Japanese could now fire effectively on the Allied cruisers, but the Allied cruisers could not return that fire.

Just after 5 P.M. Admiral Takagi ordered another torpedo attack. He was in a hurry. They had been fighting for an hour and there had been no serious damage to either side. It would soon be dusk and soon after, darkness. The Japanese were not averse to night fighting, but on this day, with their spotter planes, they knew they had a big advantage in fighting during the daylight hours. So Takagi was in a hurry.

The British cruiser *Exeter* had been a major target for the first hour and had suffered several near hits, which caused some flooding in the ship. The *Houston* had been hit by two dud shells, and the *Java* had taken a live one but was not seriously hurt.

Now, said Admiral Takagi, it was time to close with the enemy. So the Japanese destroyers headed in. The Allied cruisers fired on them, and the Japanese *Tokitsukaze* was hit. She began throwing up clouds of smoke and steam, which meant she had suffered damage to her boilers and steam system, but she kept moving and fired her eight torpedoes. So did the others—eight destroyers, each firing eight torpedoes; then they turned away while 64 torpedoes rushed toward the Allied enemy ships.

Just after five o'clock the cruiser *Exeter* was hit by an armor-piercing shell fired by the Japanese cruiser *Haguro*. The shell first struck the shield of a starboard four-inch gun and went through, killing four men of the gun crew. The armor-piercing projectile then crashed down into the boiler rooms and exploded, knocking out six of the cruiser's eight boilers and rupturing steam lines. Immediately the *Exeter* began to lose power until she could only make 11 knots.

Because she could not maintain cruising speed, the captain of the *Exeter* ordered her turned out of the battle line, and the ship turned to port. Behind her, the captain of the *Houston* saw the turn and thought a new order had been issued by the admiral. As explained earlier, communications among the Allied ships were bad. So *Houston* also turned to port; behind her the cruisers *Perth* and *Java* followed suit.

Suddenly Admiral Doorman found that much of his battle force had left him; he turned rapidly and steamed to catch up with them. When Admiral Takagi saw these maneuvers he believed the Dutch had lost heart and were running away from him, and he set off in pursuit.

As this was happening, so were other events. The swarm of torpedoes fired by the Japanese destroyers earlier now began to come to the end of their runs. One of them struck the destroyer *Kortenauer* amidships and blew the center out of her. The two ends folded up and stood up for a moment before they slid down into the sea. The Japanese destroyer *Asagumo* was also hit by a shell from one of the Allied cruisers, and her boilers were affected. She went dead in the water. But her crew managed to repair the damage and the engines were started again.

Admiral Doorman in the *De Ruyter* came up alongside the *Exeter* to ask why she had turned out of line. The captain explained that the ship could make only 15 knots at that point, and so Admiral Doorman instructed him to abandon the fight and make for safety at Surabaya. The *Exeter* headed away from the fight.

At this time Admiral Takagi was eager to end the fight because it was growing dark and the spotter planes that had provided him with such an advantage would soon be useless. He hurried to catch up to the Allied ships, and his destroyers prepared to launch another torpedo attack.

The British destroyers *Electra, Encounter,* and *Jupiter* headed back toward the enemy ships to protect the *Exeter* as she tried to get away. They were moving directly toward the oncoming Japanese cruiser *Jintsu* and her destroyers when the Japanese cruiser began firing at the *Electra*. The first few shells missed, but then the gunners got the range and the hits came rapidly. One shell hit just below the bridge; then came half a dozen more hits in swift succession. The shells blew up in the boiler rooms; the ship suddenly slowed and then came to a dead stop—her engines were gone. A Japanese destroyer came surging up and the *Electra* crew fired a spread of torpedoes at her, but all missed. The *Jintsu* and several Japanese destroyers came back and continued firing at the disabled ship. The men of the *Electra* fired back but since the Japanese shells had knocked out the firing control system, the guns had to be manned and trained by hand. The *A* turret on the *Electra* was knocked out, and then the *B* turret. The searchlight platform near the bridge was blown away. The ship began taking water swiftly, her bottom blown out, and she began to settle in the water.

The captain of the British ship saw the end coming and gave orders for the men to abandon ship. The ready ammunition for the *X* and *Y* turrets was struck by shells and began exploding. *Y* turret blew up. One boat got away from the side but was promptly hit by a shell from a destroyer and sank. A lifesaving raft was put over the side but it, too, was promptly destroyed by a Japanese shell. Men began jumping over the side and swimming away from the ship so that the suction of the sinking vessel would not drag them down. The captain, who had decided to go down with his ship, stood on the bridge and waved to them until the ship sank.

It was deep dusk now, and the battle area was largely obscured by darkness, by smoke and fires, and by the smoke screens of the Japanese destroyers.

The Japanese destroyers came into the smoke pall, and so did the Dutch and English vessels, which were protecting the retreat of the *Exeter*. The Japanese were trying to find the damaged ship, but the destroyers *Encounter* and *Jupiter* and the Dutch destroyer *Witte de With* screened the *Exeter*. The crew of the latter vessel were surprised when a terrible explosion nearly blew off their stern. It was one of their own depth charges, which had come loose and dropped over the side. The explosion also made the Japanese think the *Exeter* was hit, and in the confusion she moved off, her crew ordered by Admiral Doorman to take her back to Surabaya.

Admiral Doorman still had four cruisers—really only three and a half, since *Houston*'s after turret was missing. At least the surviving turret had eight-inch guns, which meant she was the only vessel modern enough to match the guns of the Japanese cruisers. *De Ruyter*, *Perth*, and *Java* all had six-inch guns.

The Allied cruisers came out of the smoke to find the *Nachi* and *Haguro* waiting for them. The Japanese were good shots and soon they had straddled *Houston*. That ship was in serious trouble, not only because she was a major target, but because she was nearly out of ammunition for her eight-inch guns, with less than 50 rounds for each gun. Furthermore, the forward magazines were empty, and the ammunition had to be hand carried from the after magazines to the forward guns. Still, she was fighting.

The confusion about signals continued and caused new difficulties for the Allied ships. Admiral Doorman signaled the American destroyers to counterattack, and they prepared to do so. Then he signaled them to stop the attack and make smoke, so they began to build up a smoke screen between the *De Ruyter* and the Japanese ships. Then Doorman told the Americans to cover his retreat; so, smoke pouring from their funnels, the American destroyers turned toward the Japanese ships and fired torpedoes from their starboard tubes, swung around and fired from their port tubes, and then came back toward the fleet.

One of those torpedoes hit the Japanese destroyer *Asagumo* and it slowed her down but didn't stop her. Admiral Takagi, sensing that the victory was his, told his transports, which he had kept back, to go on in and land the Japanese soldiers on the beaches of Java while he finished off the naval attack. The transports began to move.

The *Houston* was steering a strange zigzag course as the captain tried to keep his forward turret firing. The Japanese were firing on her, and two shells hit the ship, rupturing the fuel tanks. But since both shells were duds they didn't start any fires.

Admiral Doorman was now looking for the Japanese transports, meaning to strike them and stop the landing of troops. He radioed Admiral Helfrich for information, hoping that Helfrich had spotter planes out that day.

Admiral Takagi then sent the cruiser *Jintsu* and her destroyers in a great loop that would put them southeast of the convoy, thus protecting them from the Allied attack if it came.

Admiral Doorman was unable to raise his headquarters for information, so he had to guess where the Japanese transports were. He estimated they would be heading northwest of his position, and he was quite right; he then began moving in that direction. The darkness made maneuvering difficult, but it also hindered the Japanese. They still had their float planes up, though, and the planes began dropping flares, hoping to illuminate the Allied fleet for their own guns. The flares actually illuminated both fleets, which began firing at each other, but the range was too great even for the eight-inch guns. The Japanese all fired torpedoes, but the Americans were able to avoid them and they all missed their targets.

Admiral Doorman led the Allied ships in a turn to break

off contact with the Japanese, but Admiral Takagi took what he hoped was a converging course. He had no way of knowing. The float planes had run out of gas and come down. But Takagi was lucky. An hour later he came out of the darkness and saw the Allied ships far off to port in the bright moonlight.

But he didn't see all the Allied ships. The destroyer *Jupiter* had been hit by a torpedo from a Japanese submarine, and she sank. Commander Binford, the leader of the American destroyers, had decided that Doorman was taking them in too close to shore, and he broke away to head for Surabaya and refueling. The destroyer *Encounter* suddenly came upon the survivors of the destroyer *Kortenauer*, who had kept their rafts together, and she stopped to pick the men up.

When Admiral Takagi came into the bright moonlight and was seen by the Allied cruisers, he saw the four Allied cruisers were all alone.

Admiral Takagi immediately ordered a course alteration to intercept the Allied ships. The Japanese ships came forward until they were four miles from Doorman's ships. Then they launched torpedoes. One torpedo struck the *De Ruyter* aft and penetrated the signal locker; in a moment signal flares and rockets were bursting all over that section of the sea like fireworks on the Fourth of July.

The *De Ruyter* slowed down, and the *Perth*, traveling behind the *De Ruyter*, had to swerve to keep from running the flagship down, and the *Houston* had to swerve to dodge the *Perth*. Those swerves saved the ships, because the Japanese torpedoes were well aimed and would certainly have hit except for the ships maneuvering to avoid collision. One torpedo did hit the *Java*, the last in the column. In five minutes both the *Java* and the *De Ruyter* were dead in the water and burning. The fires soon reached the *De Ruyter*'s 40-mm ammunition magazine. Admiral Doorman ordered his other captains to take their ships away from the scene, to go and protect the *Batavia*. The captain of the *De Ruyter* ordered the vessel abandoned as the fires grew worse and the explosions increased. But it was too late; the *De Ruyter* and the *Java* were in desperate condition and both sank as the *Houston* and the *Perth* raced away from the scene. At the last officers begged Admiral Doorman to come away from his bridge and try to save himself, but he refused and sent them off to find whatever means of saving themselves they could. The admiral remained on his bridge as the ship sank.

Captain Waller of the *Perth* was now senior officer. He didn't have much of a fleet left and by that time it was badly scattered. He led the *Houston* toward Tanjong Priok near Batavia, where they arrived next morning. Admiral Helfrich was there and learned the sad details of Admiral Doorman's last battle.

So the battle of the Java Sea ended in another Japanese victory, one that marked the end of hopes of preventing the occupation of Java. After February 27, it was a matter of hours before the Japanese landed and began the reduction of the island's defense.

THIRTEEN

End of the Asiatic Fleet

As February 1942 came to a close, not much was left of the U.S. Asiatic fleet—the old carrier *Langley*, the battered cruiser *Houston*, a few tenders, a handful of destroyers, and a large number of submarines, which were scattered around Australia and on patrol in the waters of the Indies, sometimes successful but as often as not the victim of torpedo failure.

The *Langley* was on her way from northern Australia to Tjilatjap, carrying a deckload of 32 army air force fighter planes to help fight the battle of Java. She had sailed from Fremantle on February 23 and on February 26 was sighted by a Dutch patrol bomber not far from her destination. The *Langley*'s skipper, Commander R. P. McConnell, was looking for the American destroyers *Whipple* and *Edsall* to escort him into port. He encountered them on the morning of February 27 and joined them. At 9 A.M. the three ships were sighted by a Japanese Kawanishi flying boat, so Commander McConnell asked Admiral Glassford for air protection. Glassford, having no planes, asked Admiral Helfrich's help, and the admiral decided to use his handful of aircraft for an attack on the Japanese transports in the Java Sea.

The *Langley*, the old carrier, because of its deckload of aircraft, was a prime candidate for an attack by the Japanese air force, and they did not miss the chance. She was attacked by nine twin-engined Betty bombers, who came in at 15,000 feet and dropped their bombs. Skipper McConnell managed to avoid the first few sticks of bombs. But on the third pass, the bombers guessed right; the captain turned the *Langley* to starboard; the bombers followed and dropped seven bombs very accurately. One bomb smashed the after motorboat and started several fires. Another set fire to the planes on the flight deck. Yet another bomb smashed the port elevator aft and wrecked more planes. The planes did not explode because the gas had been drained from their tanks for the voyage, but they burned.

The fourth bomb hit near the port stack and smashed more planes. The fifth bomb hit the flight deck and started more fires, then went through onto the lower deck to start still more. The other two bombs missed.

The ship began to list to port, and the captain ordered counterflooding of the starboard compartments. The port list increased, and Commander McConnell ordered the aircraft on the port side jettisoned to lighten the ship's load.

In few minutes the engineering officer reported to the bridge that the water was four feet deep in the port motor pit. It was not long after that Commander McConnell gave the order to prepare to abandon ship. That order was to "prepare," but many young seamen panicked and began going over the side. The destroyer *Edsall* came up and began picking them out of the water. Then the *Langley*'s engines quit, drowned out.

Commander McConnell then decided to abandon the *Langley*. She was 50 miles from Tjilatjap, and she had no tug to bring her in. She was low in the water, stopped, and a prime target for the enemy. Her mission was already a failure; the planes she was to bring had almost all been destroyed. So he gave the order to abandon ship. Two boats were lowered and the wounded were put in them. Then seven life rafts and two balsa rafts were put over the side, and the rest of the men got down onto them. The last men off the ship were the executive officer and the captain. They found, after counting survivors, that all but 16 of the *Langley's* men were saved. The life boats and rafts were picked up by the destroyers, and the *Whipple* was given the task of sinking the first American aircraft carrier ever to put to sea. She sent nine shells and two torpedoes into the *Langley*, and the ship sank.

By the morning of February 28 at Tjilatjap, the Americans had learned of the sinking of the *Langley* and the departure of most of the staff of the Asiatic Fleet for Australia. Admiral Glassford remained. Everybody knew the Allies were finished in Java. Admiral Glassford closed down the port offices, and told all his people to find transportation for themselves to take them to Australia.

That day the order came to withdraw the American submarines from the bases around Java, and all ships of the American fleet were ordered out of those waters. At Surabaya, Commander Binford of American Destroyer Division 58 went ashore and telephoned Admiral Glassford. He wanted to know what to do with his four battered destroyers, which were nearly out of ammunition. Glassford told him to take the *Alden, John D. Edwards, Paul Jones,* and *John D. Ford* to Exmouth Gulf in Australia. That was supposed to be the new American base, but when Admiral Purnell arrived at Exmouth Gulf the same day he found it totally unsuitable for naval operations because of its tides and currents. So the order was rescinded and the destroyers were told to go to Fremantle, a thousand miles south, in western Australia. That was to be the new base for the Americans.

The destroyers left Java, hugging the coast as they went through the Bali Strait. They saw three Japanese destroyers, which did not see them, and escaped from Java.

One last American destroyer remained in Java waters: the *Pope*. She and the British destroyer *Encounter* were to escort the crippled cruiser *Exeter* to Ceylon for repairs. Also left behind by Allied strike force were the damaged American cruiser *Houston,* the Australian cruiser *Perth,* and the Dutch destroyer *Evertsen,* all lying together at Tandjong Priok, the naval base of Batavia.

The *Houston* was in bad shape. She had been hit and had taken so many near hits that most of the upper works were destroyed; what was not destroyed was damaged. The fire hoses leaked, the glass had broken out of the bridge windows, and the crew was exhausted from moving ammunition up from the rear ammunition rooms to the forward area.

On the morning of February 28 the *Houston* and the *Perth* made plans to refuel at Tandjong Priok, but the Dutch authorities were most unsympathetic. They told Captain Rooks of the *Houston* that they had no fuel for him; they were saving it all for the Dutch warships. And yet that same day Admiral Helfrich asked Admiral Glassford to send the *Houston* to Surabaya to join another battle with the Dutch! Admiral Glassford agreed, knowing that it would be hopeless. But his orders were to help the Dutch to the last.

So the *Houston* and the *Perth* set out for Sunda Strait, which lies between Java and Sumatra. Scout planes reported there were no Japanese forces in the vicinity; it looked like a good bet. But the scout planes had managed to miss two Japanese naval groups and 60 transports lining up to land troops on Java. So Captain Rooks of the *Houston* and the captain of the *Perth* decided to sail that night. They waited for a pilot who never showed up; finally the *Perth* led the way out through the minefield. They had thought the Dutch destroyer *Evertsen* would accompany them, but her captain had not been so informed. When the cruisers left they passed the destroyer, and her captain said he was unable to leave port at that time, his boilers were not up. So far had communications in the old ABDA command deteriorated that no one really knew what anyone else was doing. And so the two cruisers set out alone.

Outside the harbor they speeded up to 28 knots and headed for Sunda Strait, with the *Perth* in the lead.

They steamed along boldly until just before 11 P.M. when the Japanese destroyer *Fubuki* spotted them and raised the alarm. The *Fubuki* then shadowed the two ships and kept reporting on their course and speed.

The Allied ships sailed on. At 11:30 the men on the bridge of the *Houston* sighted strange ships and challenged them. There was no answer, so the Americans went to general quarters and began action. The *Perth* fired first, and the Japanese—for of course that is who it was—fired back. The first enemy ship was a destroyer, and it fired nine torpedoes at the Allied ships. They all missed, but they ran their course. Unfortunately for the Japanese their own transports were at the end of that course. That night the Japanese sank several of their own ships.

By firing star shells the *Houston* discovered she was surrounded by Japanese warships. Captain Rooks swung into the passage between Panjang Island and St. Nicholas Point to escape. But a heavy Japanese cruiser and ten destroyers lay between the *Houston* and the point, and other Japanese ships were coming up.

The *Houston* and the *Perth* did nobly. They opened fire; there were so many Japanese vessels around them that they did great damage. They sank the *Sakura Maru,* and General Imamura, the leader of the Japanese army expedition against Java, was flung into the sea. He was rescued, but several other transports were hit and many lives and much supply were lost. The *Houston* was making hits on Japanese destroyers, which were firing torpedoes that hit Japanese transports. For 50 minutes the *Houston* seemed to bear a charmed life, throwing many shells into Japanese vessels, watching them fire on each other and not taking a single shell herself.

But it could not last. The *Perth* suddenly took four torpedoes and several eight-inch shells from a cruiser simultaneously. She sank in minutes. After that all the fury of the Japanese was concentrated against the *Houston.* Three destroyers came in to attack from the stern and launched torpedoes. The captain of the *Houston* somehow managed to comb them all. But that was the end of *Houston's* luck. Two torpedoes crashed into the port side of the ship and killed every man in the after engine room. *Houston*'s speed dropped to 23 knots. One by one the guns were knocked out. A second torpedo caught her on the starboard side, and at the same time several Japanese cruisers found the range and began throwing shells into the American ship. The Number 2 turret blew up. The Number 1 turret had no more ammunition. The *Houston* was reduced to fighting with her five-inch guns, the pompoms, and the 50-caliber machine guns. But she fought on.

Japanese torpedo boats came after her, and the 50-caliber gunners took them on. One torpedo boat was sunk, but another launched a torpedo that hit the *Houston* forward. She took a strong list to starboard and became unmaneuverable. Her loudspeaker system failed. Captain Rooks called his bugler and told him to sound the call to abandon ship. The bugler blew and the men tried to get off, but the Japanese tried to stop them with an unending hail of fire from every sort of gun.

Although Captain Rooks kept urging his men to leave the ship, they could see that he had no intention of following them. Then he was hit by fragments from a Japanese shell and died in the arms of one of his officers.

More torpedoes began to hit, and the ship was literally being blown apart. Men jumped over the side, but the Japanese destroyers were nearby with their searchlights trained, and they machine-gunned the Americans in the water.

Then one last torpedo struck, and the *Houston* heeled over and sank in the waters of the Sunda Strait. The Japanese picked up about 400 of the *Houston*'s crew of 1,000, as well as crewmen from the *Perth* and the destroyer *Evertsen*, which had come out to help the cruisers after all. They were the last of the naval men of the Allied fighting ships. There was no more strike force, and there were no more surface fighting ships of the American Asiatic Fleet.

FOURTEEN

Conquest of Java

In the last days of February and the first days of March, the forces of Admiral Takagi moved around the waters of the East Indies tidying up, sinking the oiler *Pecos* and some other ships of the Allied fleet. The Allies had sent the damaged British cruiser *Exeter* under escort toward Ceylon for repairs, and she headed through the Sunda Strait.

The scout planes of the *Nachi* and the *Haguro* found the *Exeter* convoy first. Admiral Takagi was notified, and he prepared for action. He assigned Admiral Takahashi with the light cruiser *Ashigara* and the cruiser *Myoko* and two destroyers to the task. The destroyers *Pope* and *Encounter* made smoke, but there were too many Japanese ships and they were too fast for the Allied vessels. An hour after the battle opened the Japanese cruisers got the range and quickly sank the *Exeter*.

It was not long before the cruisers also sank the destroyer *Encounter*. The destroyer *Pope* managed to escape into a rain squall, turned, and when it came out of the squall found itself alone on the sea. But not for long. Soon a plane from the carrier *Ryujo* spotted the destroyer. The *Ryujo* had been busy covering the Japanese troop landings at St. Nicholas Point at the head of Sunda Strait, but that operation was near its successful end, since the strike force was no more. Six dive bombers from the carrier were sent off first; they did not do very well, scoring only a near miss, but it wrecked the port engine shaft, which slowed the destroyer down and made her easy prey for the level bombers that followed. The level bombers did not connect, however. It was left to the cruiser *Myoko* to put the finishing touch to the destroyer *Pope*. After the *Myoko* had fired six salvoes the *Pope* went down, stern first.

By March 1 the Japanese were overrunning Java, and General Imamura was having no difficulty achieving his military objectives one by one. By March 1 the Japanese were only 50 miles from Batavia.

The British and American naval commands abandoned Java on March 2. There were no ships left; British Admiral Palliser and American Admiral Glassford traveled by PBY patrol bomber to Australia.

On land, the Japanese victory was as stunning and swift as it had been on the sea and in the air. The simple fact was that the Japanese forces overwhelmed the Allies because they were better trained and better disciplined and their commanders knew precisely what they were doing.

General Imamura's army of 25,000 men had completely defeated the Dutch army of 100,000. One reason for Japanese victory was the reluctance of the Indonesian troops to fight for the Dutch; another was the belief of many of the Indonesians that the Japanese plan of Asia for the Asians was the way of the future.

On March 7, so rapidly had victory come, General Tojo called a liaison conference between the government and Imperial General Headquarters to decide a policy toward prisoners, internees, and the future of Japanese expansion. It seemed unbelievable, but with the exception of a handful of enemy forces still fighting a faltering rearguard action in Burma and the Americans still holding out on Bataan and Corregidor in the Philippines, all the objectives established by the Japanese in 1941 had been achieved.

The Japanese had defeated the British-Indian forces in a

battle near Rangoon and were occupying the city. The British were retreating through central Burma toward the Chindwin River. No further Japanese offensive action was contemplated anywhere until the completion of the Thai-Burma railroad.

At Tojo's meeting it was decided that the railroad would be built by Allied prisoners of war. There could be no coddling of the prisoners of war, said General Tojo. They would have to earn their keep. Thus was established the Japanese policy of slave labor toward the POWs that was to lead to the deaths of so many thousands of prisoners and ultimately to the conviction and hanging of General Tojo for war crimes.

At the meeting it was also decided that a naval strike would be made against the British Eastern Fleet, based at Trincomalee in Ceylon. That was the only force in Asian waters now capable of dealing any blow to Japan.

The navy now suggested that the next step in Japanese empire building should be the capture of Hawaii and Australia. The army rejected that proposal; both occupations would have to be carried out by the army, and the lines of communication would be too long. As General Tojo reminded everyone, all that they had done so far had been to facilitate the settlement of the China incident. Once China was under control, all the other territories would fall neatly into place. There was really no need to go farther afield.

What needed to be done now, said General Tojo, was to delineate the outer perimeter of the empire and to be sure that the means of settlement and protection were available. The question was raised about the American potential to make war against Japan. It would not be ready to do so until December 1943, the earliest the American fleet could be rebuilt, said the navy. But the Americans might make air raids against Japan from the Aleutian Islands with long-range bombers.

All agreed it was unthinkable that the Americans should bomb Japan but that some precautions should be taken nonetheless. Army and navy would cooperate to capture New Caledonia, Fiji, Samoa, British New Guinea, and the Aleutian Islands. This would guarantee the safety of the East Indies and Japan proper. The first attacks would be made against British New Guinea, or Papua, as it was called. The Japanese would seize the city of Port Moresby and then take the rest of the area. Then, in early June, they would send a force to the Aleutian Islands to establish bases and prevent the Americans from using the islands to launch attacks against Japan. As a sop to the navy, a plan to seize Midway Island was also included. Admiral Yamamoto wanted to take Midway to draw the American fleet out from Pearl Harbor and finish the job bungled by Admiral Nagumo in December: the destruction of the American carrier force. His staff also wanted to discuss a future attack on Hawaii, but Yamamoto was still of the belief that unless Japan could negotiate with America soon, ultimately Japan would lose the war. Thus he was in a hurry to win a big naval victory and then get to the peace table.

All this was revealed to the Japanese people in a newspaper interview given by Rear Admiral Tanetsuga Sosa, in which he indicated that the Aleutians would be attacked at the beginning of June, and that the Japanese also planned to attack the Australian coastal cities because the Americans had moved their Asiatic Fleet submarines there. He also forecast the coming raid on Trincomalee by the Combined Fleet Carrier Strike Force under Admiral Nagumo.

A week later the first move of the new program took place: the bombing of Port Moresby by Japanese aircraft and the invasion of the villages of Lae and Salamaua on Papua by army troops, who met only slight opposition from native scouts.

Within two weeks after March 1, all Java was secure, but General Imamura faced an enormous problem: what was to be done with the thousands of prisoners of war and civilian detainees who had suddenly fallen under his control. The prisoners were brutally treated; many were killed out of hand, as had a band of women who were marched by soldiers straight into the sea and drowned. There were two reasons for the Japanese mistreatment of European prisoners of war and civilian noncombatants. First, the logistic reason: the Japanese victories had been so swift there was no time for the military to bring in administrators to handle the civilians. Second, and far more important, was the whole Japanese approach to the world. In their view, "Dai Nippon," Great Japan, was the most important power in the world. The Europeans were monsters who had been enslaving and mistreating the people of Asia for generations. Now it was Asia's turn, and the Europeans (including Americans) must be humiliated. To humiliate them, the Japanese tortured them and killed them, raped the women and disemboweled the men—and all this was done before native audiences so that they would be impressed with Japanese power.

On Java, a Japanese army propagandist named Tomojo Abe put the picture in Japanese perspective:

Abe had gone into the town of Galu, about 50 miles from Bandoeng, and there he had found 5,000 Dutch, British, Australian, and American prisoners of war, all inside a barbed-wire barricade hurriedly erected by General Imamura's troops. Each nationality had its own set of barracks. Abe had some respect for the Australians and the British, who were tough and refused to answer his questions. But he had nothing but contempt for the Americans. They were soft people, he said.

"I visited the Americans and was astonished. As soon as they saw me the American officers sprang forward and began bowing and scraping before me. Although I did not ask them any questions they vied with one another in telling me about their past records and life histories. I was disgusted with them."

"I picked out one young officer and asked him, 'Are you a bachelor?'"

"The officer immediately pulled out a picture of a woman, his sweetheart, from his pocket, and jabbering something excitedly, he began to weep copiously. . . ."

This sort of anecdote was faithfully reprinted in the Japanese daily newspapers in the spring of 1942. The purpose, as with photographs of white men sweeping the streets of Singapore and other towns while natives looked on with glee, of columns of white prisoners, wending their way wretchedly toward prison camps, of crowds of white civilians, ragged and dirty, moving from one camp to another—all this was designed to bring down the white man in the eyes of Asians and to prove the superiority of the Japanese.

The fact was that the Japanese did not really believe they were truly superior to the white men, and because they did not believe it they tried all the harder to convince themselves.*

In Indonesia, General Imamura moved swiftly and efficiently to establish a government of local participation, which was designed to appeal to the Indonesians. He brought Achmed Sukarno out of a Dutch jail and offered him the leadership of the Indonesian government if he would cooperate with the Japanese. Sukarno, who had no reason to love the white man and no reason to hate the Japanese, agreed, with the proviso that he would be free to choose his own course of action once the war was ended and the white men were driven out of Asia for good. Imamura then chose a governing council of 15, 10 Indonesians and five Japanese, and turned the civil government over to them. Of course, the Japanese army stood sentinel to this government, but as far as the Indonesians were concerned, they were running their own affairs.

*The Japanese still differentiate people according to race, even within nations. A close Japanese friend of mine came to America and was particularly interested in differences between white people and other Americans. I asked the question, "Do you Japanese feel inferior to white people?" The answer: "Yes, we really do. We don't admit it, but we really do."

It was the most freedom they had ever known. The new Republic of Indonesia was proclaimed a successful star in the firmament of the Greater East Asia Coprosperity Sphere.

FIFTEEN

The Fall of Bataan

The Bataan Peninsula and Corregidor still were bastions of the American presence in the Philippines in the early months of 1942, and each week that presence rankled the Imperial General Staff more and more.

Actually, although General Honma was to take the blame, the fault lay with Imperial General Headquarters itself. In its eagerness to gather the harvest of the Dutch East Indies, the military oligarchy had deprived General Honma of the Forty-eighth Division. So he was fighting the battle of Bataan with about a third as many troops as the Americans and Filipinos had combined. But time was on Honma's side. If his men fell ill they could be withdrawn from the battle for awhile. The Americans and Filipinos were there on the peninsula, barricaded, but they were unable to move. Increasingly they suffered from disease and exhaustion, and finally hunger also began to cut them down.

With the evacuation of Cavite and Manila, the American naval forces moved to Mariveles at the tip of the Bataan Peninsula and to the fortress island of Corregidor, just off the tip. On Corregidor they lived in tunnels, along with the army staff of General MacArthur and specialists.

The navy did some fighting of its own. One night that winter Lieutenant Commander John D. Bulkeley in *PT–41* torpedoed a Japanese transport. Lieutenant Malcolm Champlin of the navy went ashore on Bataan to become liaison between the navy and the army. His main job was to get information that would help the PT boats and the submarines carry on the sea war against the Japanese.

At the end of January the submarine *Seawolf* arrived with 37 tons of antiaircraft ammunition, the first supply the men of the Philippines had received. On the night of February 3, the submarine *Trout* came in from Pearl Harbor, bringing more antiaircraft ammunition. She then took out the Philippine government's gold and silver reserves. A few hours later the submarine *Seadragon* came in and took out a number of radiomen and other specialists.

As March came, the men of the fleet and those of the army were wearing down. A thousand sailors were still at Mariveles. In Washington the decision was made to bring General MacArthur out of the Philippines. The reason was the MacArthur name: he had been chief of staff of the army and was the best-known soldier in America, and his name was not to be associated with an American defeat. President Roosevelt announced that MacArthur would go to Australia and reorganize the American military effort against Japan. So MacArthur and Admiral Rockwell, the senior naval officer present; the MacArthur family; and some members of MacArthur's staff set out in four of the PT boats for the southern Philippines. They made it to the coast of Mindanao, where they boarded two B–17 bombers and were flown to Australia.

General Jonathan Wainwright thus became the commander who would have to fight as long as possible and then finally surrender to the Japanese.

By mid-March, supplies were growing low on Bataan. The Americans were running out of medical supplies, and hundreds of men were suffering from malaria and dysentery. Every day the Japanese air force came over, and almost every day a few yards were lost on the defense line.

On March 16 the submarine *Permit* came to Corregidor and picked up Lieutenant Champlin, Admiral Rockwell's aide; a number of army nurses; and some more specialists such as code experts.

In Tokyo in mid-March the pressure grew greater; Imperial General Headquarters pointed out to General Honma that the Dutch East Indies had now fallen and there was no further serious resistance against Japan in the Pacific except in the Philippines, which was becoming an embarrassment.

Indeed, the Americans in the Philippines were making life miserable for the Japanese. The three gunboats from China, the *Mindanao*, the *Oahu*, and the *Luzon*, discovered a flotilla of Japanese small boats and barges ferrying supplies out of Cavite on the night of March 25. The gunboats ran in and raised havoc, sinking six boats and tugs.

By this time, the food and medical supplies of the Americans in the Philippines hit a new low. On Corregidor the Americans were subsisting largely on rice, with a few canned tomatoes.

The Japanese sent aircraft that dropped leaflets addressed to General Wainwright:

Proclamation:

Bataan Peninsula is about to be swept away. Important points of southern Luzon between Ternate and Nasugbu are in the hands of the Japanese forces, and the mouth of Manila Bay is under complete control of the Japanese navy. Hopes for the arrival of reinforcements are quite in vain. The fate of Corregidor Island is sealed.

If you continue to resist the Japanese forces will by every possible means destroy and annihilate your forces relentlessly, to the last man.

This is your final chance to cease resistance. Further resistance is completely useless.

Your commander will sacrifice every man and in the end will surrender in order to save his life.

You, dear soldiers, take it into consideration. Give up your arms and stop resistance at once.

Commander in chief of the Imperial Japanese forces.

On March 23, General Honma addressed a communication calling on General Wainwright to surrender. No reply was given.

The Americans on Bataan were starving. At the end of March they were reduced to eating lizards. As one officer said, looking around at his companions, "They looked like walking dead." They ate rice and fish if they were lucky. Most of them had malaria, and the supply of quinine was virtually exhausted. Almost all of them had diarrhea, if not dysentery. Hunger tended to bring out the worst in the officers and men. The men knew that some officers were trading cartons of cigarettes to the navy men for sugar, fruit juice, and jams. The officers kept those supplies in their quarters and would not share them. One officer said they would rather throw the goods into the sea than share, but when an enlisted man put his .45 Colt automatic on the table and told the officer to think about that a little bit, the jams and jellies began to appear.

Human frailty did not change the equation. Little by little the Americans were being worn down by the Japanese; the Americans were bombed and fought on the line every day, while the unremitting pressure of Japanese might was never turned off.

At the end of March the Japanese increased their pressure as Imperial General Headquarters demanded a victory. Reinforcements were coming in for the Japanese almost every day. More than 20,000 fresh troops, as well as more planes and field guns, arrived.

By April 1 the Japanese had replaced the sick troops in their line with fresh soldiers, and they were ready to start a final offensive. The offensive began on April 3, against Mount Samat just behind the center of the Bagao-Orion line, with a five-hour artillery barrage.

On April 5 fighting was intense as the Japanese poured fresh shock troops into the line and the weary Americans and Filipinos resisted them. The Japanese artillery was their most effective weapon. The Japanese sent thousands of rounds of artillery fire into an area not more than a mile deep. All day long Japanese planes flew over the battle line, bombing and strafing. One by one the Americans lost guns, trucks, radios, all their equipment. Stubbornly the Americans resisted, giving up ground by the foot, forming into groups that represented three or four different units and continuing to fight.

On April 7 the United States War Department issued a communiqué, one that indicated how close the end was:

"Superior enemy forces, supported by tanks and artillery, continue to attack the center of our line in Bataan. The Japanese have thrown fresh reserves into the fighting and have made some additional progress. Heavy losses had been sustained by our forces. Japanese dive bombers are assisting the attack, dropping bombs and machine gunning our front line soldiers."

So the Mount Samat line broke, and the Americans started back through the foothills. The Japanese came after them with their artillery.

One enlisted man recalled the scene:

"We were ordered to counterattack. What we were going to counterattack with, I have no earthly idea. But these were our orders. Our officers met in a clump of trees and I was standing nearby. The Japanese put a round right in the trees. Plump! I don't know how many were killed. It blew me down and away. When I got up, I got up running. . . ."

By April 8 the situation had become hopeless. It was obvious that the Japanese were in a hurry to end it; their bombers kept coming over the lines, wave after wave, to be followed by fighter planes. Nothing was safe. A bus came up to take wounded Americans and Filipinos to the rear, loaded up, started back, and was hit by a bomb that killed every man on board. If it had gotten back to the hospital the men would have found there was no room for them. There were no more beds. One patient would be sleeping on the springs, one on the mattress, and one on the stuffed mattress covers.

Hospital No. 1 was bombed that day. A 500-pound bomb was dropped directly on the hospital, killing and wounding many patients.

The American defense was fast disintegrating. One captain decided to set up a defense line along the Alangan ridge, but since he had no shovels, he looked for a natural defensive position. While he was looking, his battalion was worked over by half a dozen Japanese planes. He sent his men past the ridge to the woods beyond, but many of them did not make it; they were bombed and strafed by the Japanese planes.

That night a group of 14 officers came through the captain's position, and urged him to go with them to Corregidor instead of remaining with his troops. The captain told them they had an obligation to stay with the men. They laughed at him. He said that if he survived the war he would have them courtmartialed. They went on, heading to Corregidor.

That night many of the men were on top of the mountain on the road that zigzags down into Mariveles.

On the Manila Bay side of Bataan the 120th and 515th Antiaircraft regiments got orders to destroy all their heavy equipment and fall back to Cabcaben Airfield. The line they formed was about a mile long, manned by 1,500 men. They expected attack by ten times that number the next day.

The War Department communiqué of April 8 termed the Japanese attack the "longest sustained drive of the enemy since operations began on Bataan."

That same night, April 8, the army nurses at Hospital No. 1 and Hospital No. 2 were told they would be evacuated to Corregidor. They were hustled aboard buses and cars and taken down to Mariveles to wait for boats to Corregidor. Down on the beach, the late arrivals found the boats had already gone. They hid on the beach under concrete wreckage until finally boats came to pick them up. That night the fighting reached Hospital No. 2, which was supposed to be way behind the lines. The American line was almost completely disorganized, units were all mixed up, and there was virtually no coherence left in the defenses. Besides, there was practically nothing left to defend. The Americans had been pushed back almost to the tip of Bataan. From that point, the Americans began blowing up ammunition dumps and all the equipment they could find. It was very near the end of the line.

Then came April 9. The troops were down in the Mariveles area, at the end of the peninsula. There was no place else to go. At 3:30 in the morning, officers representing General King, the commander of the Bataan force, made their way under a white flag to the Japanese lines, prepared to surrender. A few hours later the force surrendered unconditionally to the Japanese.

General Wainwright had already made his way to Corregidor, and from Fort Mills on that island sent a message to the War Department, telling them the Japanese had succeeded in enveloping the east flank of the lines. It was a confused, incoherent report, but it was understood in Washington. On April 10 Washington announced the fall of Bataan, and Secretary of War Henry Stimson said he did not know the fate of the defenders, except that "they apparently face death or surrender."

Indeed they did. Here is an account, by Captain Mark Wohlfield, of those first moments after the surrender:

"Soon we heard a lot of hubbub at the forward end of the line, way ahead of us around the bend in the road, and we saw our first Japanese. The first ones were artillery men carrying a mountain howitzer. They were cheerful-looking little fellows, and they smiled as they walked by. They were all covered with sweat, and we were amazed at the weight they carried. One carried a wheel, another the tube, another the trail, another the packs of the fellows carrying the piece. They all had flies around their heads. Having been in the jungle for awhile they were filthy.

"After them came the infantry, and they were a lot more vicious. They started to go through our pockets. Some knew a little English and hollered 'Go you to Hell. Go you to Hell!' One of the Japs went over to Colonel Sewell and showed him that he wanted the colonel to take off his wedding ring. Sewell kept refusing. About that time a Jap came up to me and cleaned me out. Then he reached into my back pocket. Suddenly he jumped back and the bayonet came up real fast between my eyes. I reached into my pocket and found a rifle clip I'd forgotten about. Quickly I dropped it to the ground. The Jap took his rifle and cracked me across the head. I fell. My head was covered with blood. When I looked up I saw Sewell couldn't get his wedding ring off, and the Jap was about to take his bayonet and cut it off along with the finger. Sewell saw me and he reached over to get some of my blood, which he used to wiggle the ring off. Then he was slapped and kicked.''

How the Americans were treated depended on the Japanese involved. One captain of the Philippine Scouts was picked up by a Japanese squad that kept him with them all day, fed him, and treated him very well, although, of course, they took his wristwatch and jewelry.

A sergeant encountered a Japanese officer who spoke beautiful English. He welcomed the Americans, gave them cigarettes, and after they had smoked them he beat the Americans. Then he marched them off to join a larger group.

One Japanese told another American captain:

"You are going to find a lot of bad Japanese and you are going to find a lot of good ones. Please don't think that all the Japanese are alike as far as the treatment you are going to receive is concerned.'' That particular Japanese gave the captain a can of sardines and some rice. It was the first real food the captain had eaten in several days.

Others were beaten, kicked, and insulted. But one thing some of them noted was that the Japanese were as tough with their own people as they were with the Americans. One American private noted that the first Japanese soldiers he met were bone tired infantrymen who marched past the prisoners as they waited beside the road. One Japanese private was so tired he stumbled and fell. An officer saw him fall in front of the Americans and barked an order, whereupon two other soldiers picked up the Japanese private and took him off the road where the Americans could not see what happened. The Americans heard a shot, and the two Japanese soldiers returned alone.

For the first hour or two nothing much happened to the prisoners. Then the Japanese troops began taking the Americans down out of the mountains in groups to Little Baguio on the road out of Mariveles and moving them up the road in groups of a hundred men or so. All the Americans and Filipinos sensed that something else was about to happen.

SIXTEEN

Death March

The Japanese had been ill informed about what they would find on Bataan Peninsula. They believed the American and Filipino troop contingents would amount to 40,000 or 50,000 men. When Imperial General Headquarters began to grow impatient with General Honma they sent their favorite goad, Lieutenant Colonel Tsuji, to the Philippines. He arrived with a plan for the evacuation of the Bataan Peninsula once it was captured, so that the Japanese troops could get on with the capture of Corregidor fortress.

But the Japanese were extremely short of motor transportation. So the plan called for the Allied prisoners of war to be marched out of the peninsula, to Dinalupihan, to Lubao, to Guagua, and finally to San Fernando where the rail line began. From there they would be taken to Camp O'Donnell and organized.

On the morning of April 9, when the sun came up on Bataan, the Japanese senior officers saw with dismay what an enormous task they faced in moving out all the prisoners, since there were more than 70,000, not 40,000, as Homma had devoutly hoped. Until the Japanese could get the prisoners out of the way, the siege of Corregidor could not get under way; as long as Corregidor held out, the Japanese believed, the world would see that the Americans were still fighting in the Philippines, and the reorganization of the Philippine government and economy to serve Japan could not begin.

So the morning sun came up on a scene of total confusion at Mariveles. Tanks, trucks, men, cars, horses, and field guns, both American and Japanese, were all mixed together. The weather was hot, and dust blew over everything. Before many hours had passed, the Japanese learned that most of their prisoners were sick and that to march them the 60 miles from Mariveles to San Fernando was going to be a herculean task. This knowledge did not make the Japanese happy, and they reacted in different ways. The initial reaction, that of such men as Lieutenant Colonel Tsuji, was anger because their plans had miscarried, and such men immediately took out their resentments on the prisoners.

The Japanese gathered the Americans into groups of 100 and marched them along. As the men moved it got hotter and they grew tired very quickly, since most of them were suffering from malaria. Many prisoners began to falter. When that happened it was the end for them. Once a man fell out of line, the guards began prodding him with their bayonets, then they would stab him, and then they would shoot him.

The first groups of prisoners were used for propaganda. The guards stopped them near a battery of 155-mm howitzers and turned them over to a crew of cameramen from the Domei news agency and reporters. The prisoners were arranged in groups and seated on the cannon so the photographers could take their pictures.

The first night, this group stopped in a rice field and sat. They didn't sleep, they just sat. Occasionally a Japanese column would go by, and sometimes a Japanese soldier would fall out of line to smack a prisoner with his rifle butt, and then rush back to the line.

One prisoner, on crutches because of a leg injury, was having trouble keeping up. He began lagging behind, and when he reached kilometer post 147 he knew he was not going to make it. His friends urged him to keep going, because in their group noses were counted at check points. And if a man was missing, so rumor had it, the Japanese would shoot 10 men.

He never found out whether or not the rumor was true.

A Japanese guard forced one sick prisoner to carry the Japanese soldier's pack. The prisoner faltered on the second day, and the Japanese picked up his rifle as if to shoot him. Another American quickly took the pack and carried it all that day. The Japanese soldier seemed appreciative and gave him some water and crackers. Other Americans called the soldier "ass kisser." His answer was that he had saved an American's life by doing it.

That night they rested on the highway. Next morning the Japanese soldier and his pack were gone.

Most of the Americans tried to protect their buddies, but if a man fell out, there was nothing that could be done for him.

Time became blurred. Everything became meaningless. Only motion counted. One American threw away his tent half, then his pistol belt, then his mosquito netting, first cutting out a piece just large enough to cover his face and hands when he lay down. Not carrying too much weight was one vital consideration, getting water was another. This prisoner saved his canteen and virtually nothing else.

The prisoners were not allowed to stop to get water, no matter how great their thirst. One time the same American broke ranks when he saw a well. A Japanese soldier yelled at him. The American, knowing he would get one end of the rifle or the other, either a blow with the butt or a bayonet in the back, ran and hid at the back of the village. Then he made a wide circle and rejoined the column. The Japanese didn't bother him. He got no water, but neither was he killed.

A few of the Americans were lucky. The Japanese had earmarked some transportation for the prisoners, but they did not have nearly enough, so they used whatever they could. General Honma, preparing for the siege of Corregidor, was sending trucks full of equipment to Mariveles.

On the way back the now-empty trucks would stop and pick up prisoners and take them as far as Capas, where the trucks were to pick up more equipment. Those prisoners were lucky, even if they were jammed into the trucks like cordwood.

On the road the jammed trucks would pass marching columns of prisoners, some of whom would try to cling to the sides of the trucks, but the trucks moved too fast. Since there was no room inside, the men fell off; they would pick themselves up and begin to march again.

After the second day many men began to fall back and then fall out. Those who fell out were shot or bayoneted. Most of the young men managed to keep going, but most of the older men fell out.

Some Japanese were kind. Three prisoners, two of them half carrying their friend, found a hut on a hillside and stopped. Six Japanese were inside. The Americans thought they would be killed, but the Japanese not only let them alone, they let the prisoners get water.

But if a particular officer or chief noncommissioned officer was a sadist—and the Japanese army system made sadists of many of them—the prisoners suffered. One group of 100 men was marched to a big artesian well where a four-inch pipe was connected up so that water flowed plentifully. The prisoners were marched up to the well, stopped, and told to stand at attention. Any prisoner who moved toward the well was shot or bayoneted, and the bodies were left where they fell. By the third day the bodies were stinking. All along the road were corpses—swollen, burst open, and with maggots crawling all over them. No one could identify the bloated, blackened corpses.

One group, under the control of a sadist, was fed three times on the march. Each time the men were marched past an open gasoline drum full of hot rice. A Japanese cook would ladle some rice into their open hands. A few feet farther on another Japanese would sprinkle it with salt. The men then ate what they could from their hands.

Another sadist made his prisoners march at double time

part of the way. When some fell out, soldiers at the back of the column shot them down. The most abusive, the men of this column found, were the Koreans. Apparently they felt they had to prove themselves to the Japanese, who did not like them. The Koreans were not fighting troops but service troops, and they were the most sadistic.

At night, if the prisoners were lucky, their guards found a warehouse for them to sleep in. If they were unlucky they were put inside a barbed-wire enclosure, used night after night for new groups of prisoners. They were not allowed to dig latrines. The whole enclosure by the third day became a mess of feces and urine and stench.

At daylight the prisoners would be awakened, told to get up, and formed into columns of four. If the chief guard was humane, they would be allowed to get water. If not, they suffered.

In one column the men devised a plan to help their fellows. The weakest men would start the day at the head of the column. As they weakened further and tended to fall back, others would help them until they grew too tired. Then they would pass the weakened prisoners back toward the rear of the column. If the weak ones got to the end and could not march any farther—the others would hear the shots.

One soldier had been wounded during previous action and had a small piece of shrapnel in his leg. It became infected and he found the going harder every day. On the third night a man crawled up to his group and whispered that he was a doctor. The soldier told him about the shrapnel. A Japanese guard came up and the doctor asked if he could take the shrapnel out. The guard first ran to the road to see if anyone was watching, then came back and permitted the operation. The soldier passed out. The doctor removed the shrapnel and wrapped a dirty towel around the leg.

That night the Japanese soldier took care of the wounded American prisoner. Next morning the guard and his whole squad were gone.

The wounded man's group was then marched along by

new guards. They came to a river. The bridge had been destroyed by the retreating Americans, but the Japanese had put up an engineer's bridge. However, only the Japanese troops used the bridge. The Americans had to march to the river and then across it. They were warned not to try to drink any water on the way across. Some men trailed towels in the water and got some moisture that way. On the bridge lounged a group of Japanese soldiers, laughing at the weak efforts of the Americans to climb the bank. When one stopped and cupped his hands to get a drink, a Japanese on the bridge shot him.

Why this emphasis on deprivation of water, thirst, and punishment? For one thing, the Japanese intended to force the Americans into absolute discipline, absolute obedience, and abject submission. For another, if the men were allowed to stop to drink they would slow down the march.

One prisoner, a cavalryman, was wearing his heavy cavalry boots and had no other shoes. The boots formed blisters on his feet and weighed him down. Finally he grew so weak that two friends had to support him, half dragging him as they marched. Someone shouted, "Here comes a guard!" The two friends tried to drag the cavalryman off the road for a moment, but the guard was too quick. He came up, jammed his bayonet through the cavalryman's body, pulled it out, and went away. The friends dropped the body and moved back into the column.

Another American, looking down at the dusty ground, saw the perfect imprint of a human foot. One foot, not two. And then he saw another single footprint farther up the road. What could this be? Finally, he saw a man ahead of him with blood running down one leg to the ground, where it made a perfect print of one foot. And then the man dropped back....

At a night camp, an American went to a water spigot. A Japanese soldier saw him and bayoneted him. The Japanese and one of his fellow soldiers dragged the American to a Japanese latrine trench and pushed him in. The American's arm came up. They pushed it down. It came up again. They pushed it down again with their bayonets. The American literally drowned in feces.

On the third day an American sergeant grew too weak to go any farther. He lay down by the side of the road and waited, expecting to be killed as he had seen so many others killed. A Japanese officer came up and moved the American into the shade of a tree. He told the American to rest. He had food brought to the American, who was too sick to eat it. The officer stayed in the area for three days for some reason the American could not understand. Then he told the American to move. The American stalled. The officer said he would kill the American if he did not move. The American moved. He never saw the officer again.

Lieutenant Colonel Tsuji came down to the line to see how the march was going. He saw an American soldier moving slowly, pulled out his samurai sword, and struck the man down. "That's how to deal with these bastards," Tsuji said.

The prisoners had a grapevine that passed word from one group to another, and they learned to drop off the road whenever a column of trucks came toward Corregidor. The trucks carried Japanese troops going into battle, and they would lean out of their trucks with bamboo poles or knotted ropes and strike at the prisoners as they passed.

One sight mentioned by many prisoners was that of a man who had been run over by a tank; his body had been left in the road. Those who passed it early in the march saw a body that had been smashed. Those who passed it later saw nothing but a mass of flesh and blood.

At Lubao, a particularly sadistic Japanese leader herded one group of prisoners into a sheet-iron warehouse for the night. The doors and windows were all closed, although it was very hot. Many of the men were very weak, and the Japanese decided to dispose of the weak ones the next day. The Japanese dug a big hole. Next morning they told the men to get up. Those who had suffered so much from the heat during the night they could not get up were thrown into the hole. Some men who tried to crawl out of the warehouse were knocked in the head and then thrown into the hole—alive or dead. It didn't matter.

Other prisoners, who spent the night in the sugar cane fields managed to get pieces of cane to chew. Yet others who were kept overnight in the sweet potato fields were able to carry off a few sweet potatoes. This meager fare of sugar cane and sweet potatoes helped some Americans survive.

The next day at Orani, halfway to San Fernando where the trains would be, a group of Americans who had made it that far were forced to sit in the sun for several hours. A number of the men collapsed. Somehow they attracted the attention of a friendly Japanese officer who moved them into a medical shack. The day after, a Japanese truck convoy returning from the Corregidor area stopped at Orani, picked up the sick, and took them to San Fernando.

After the marchers reached the mainland of Luzon, some began to escape, assisted by Filipinos. Until then escape had been impossible, but now there was some place to run to, and many Filipino people helped the Americans. A soldier and a chaplain for instance, took advantage of a cloud of dust that had blown across the road to break away from the forced march. They hid against a hedge all day. That night a young Filipino boy who had seen them came for them and led them through a nearby marsh to a creek. From there the Americans were taken by dugout canoe into the interior and safety.

The prisoners on the forced march finally reached San Fernando, where they were loaded into trains. The Japanese had divided them into groups—100 men to a boxcar, the same sort of railroad car the French had used to transport 40 men or eight horses in World War I. Because of the crowding, the American prisoners were forced to stand.

The trains stopped occasionally during the trip and the Japanese guards would open the doors so the men could get some air. They would take the dead ones out then: the prisoners would pass the bodies along above their heads to the door and then out . . . .

The trains finally arrived at Capas, where the boxcar doors were opened and the prisoners ordered out. They were told to sit down and were counted. While the prisoners from the train were being counted, they were joined by those who had been transported by truck and those who had had to march all the way. After all the prisoners had been assembled at Capas, they were marched the last eight miles to Camp O'Donnell, the airfield left unfinished by the Americans, who also partially destroyed the water resource. The Japanese had taken over the camp and decided to use it to house the prisoners until Corregidor surrendered.

There were no medical facilities or supplies at the airfield except for what little, if anything, the American doctors had managed to bring with them. The Japanese gave the Americans no medical assistance. At least, though, the Bataan death march had ended. And although other horrors were in store for those who survived, the very worst of it was over.

SEVENTEEN

Japan's War

The mood of Japan was euphoric in the extreme and had been since the first week of the war. For four years the people of Japan had been prepared for war; indeed, they actually had been at war in China during those years, although the government never called it anything but "the China incident" and pretended it would be resolved at any moment. It *was* a pretense, because by 1938 the Japanese knew that Chiang Kai-shek would never reach an accommodation with them, nor would he surrender. But General Tojo and the other military men continued to delude themselves that ultimately they could defeat China and take it over. There lay the root of everything that had happened in the Pacific; if Japan was to triumph over China she had to have the resources of Southeast Asia.

By the end of the first week of the war the newspapers had already begun boasting that the Japanese successes were marvelous, which from the Japanese viewpoint they were, but they were unexpected as well. Many naval officers had privately predicted that Admiral Yamamoto's carrier strike on Pearl Harbor would fail miserably. But when Washington announced the sinking of four American battleships, the doubting Thomases were silenced.

For a time the grand success at Pearl Harbor was the

favorite topic of Japanese artists, and the newspapers were full of artists' conceptions of burning ships and low-flying Japanese planes whizzing by above them.

The major Tokyo newspapers put aside their intensive competition long enough to sponsor jointly a rally, "To Crush the United States and Britain," at Korakuen Stadium. A new superpatriotic front was created that day, called the Neighborhood Associations. But there was more than just patriotism to the associations. Their formation was part of a government plan to enlist all the people in the war effort. The Neighborhood Associations would be responsible for their members' contributions to the war effort and later, for such air raid protection as they were able to provide.

Now, in the early days of the war, everything foreign, which had once been so prized by the Japanese, was to be discarded. Gone were the days when the Meiji and Taisho ladies aped the styles of Paris and London. Gone were the Japanese gentleman who drank champagne and his lady who wore a flapper dress in imitation of the fashions and lifestyles of New York. Gone were the days when the sexy Hollywood actress was queen of the Ginza as well. Newspaper editorialists inveighed against foreign habits, foreign clothing, foreign cars, foreign perfumes. Anything Western had once been desirable; now, anything Western was bad. A fashionable lady walking on the Ginza in high heels and Western dress was booed by passersby who pointed to a woman clopping along in wooden *geta* beneath her kimono and shouted at the Westernized lady that that was the way Japanese women should live. A reporter for *Mainichi Shimbun* chronicled it all.

Within two weeks after the start of the war, the fashionable ladies of the Ginza had all disappeared. Foreign restaurants languished. Sales of Scotch whiskey and other foreign delicacies virtually stopped. French cheeses rotted in the foreign delicatessens. Motion picture houses quietly substituted Japanese films for foreign films.

The hate-Westerners campaign gained momentum every day. This was not accidental but a part of General Tojo's effort to spur development of the Greater East Asia Co-prosperity Sphere, which was designed to become a major element in the shoring up of the Japanese war economy. The other nations—Thailand, Wang Ching-wei's Nanking puppet regime in China, and Manchukuo—were now to be strengthened by the capture of Philippines, Malaya, and, the Japanese government hoped, the Dutch East Indies.

All during December of 1941, the government trumpeted its successes as if scarcely believing them themselves. Indeed, the senior officers of the Japanese army and navy were virtually shellshocked by the ease with which their forces slashed through the Western defenses. A few, like Admiral Yamamoto, were sickened by the excesses of the propagandists, but even Yamamoto's great fame was not enough to protect him in these times, should he choose to voice his criticism. He knew it and, except to a handful of intimates, said nothing about his conviction that the war was bound to turn out badly for the Japanese, particularly now that Admiral Nagumo had failed to destroy the U.S. Pacific Fleet. While the men around Yamamoto were loudly praising Japan's successes, he was warning that the Westerners had not yet begun to fight. But his warnings were uttered too quietly to be heard.

Since January 1942, with the fall of Hong Kong, the sinking of two mighty British warships, and the rapid advance of the Japanese down the Malay Peninsula, Japan's propagandists were beside themselves with glee. The Japanese army was a super army, they said. The Japanese soldier was superman. The Japanese soldiers were like gods, and of course no effete Westerners could stand up against these gods.

Every day the major newspapers were filled with articles lauding the efforts of the Japanese fighting men. Radio Tokyo broadcast every few hours, interviewing captured foreign soldiers and quoting them as being in awe of the power of Japan and overwhelmed by the generosity of their captors. Meanwhile, the "generous" captors were beating and starving and sometimes murdering the captives for the delectation of the native populations of the conquered countries.

For the most part the natives were *pictured* as ecstatic, as on Guam, where "people greeted the coming of the Japanese with joy." Certainly there were millions of the colonial peoples who did feel this way after hundreds of years of European repression. But there were also many millions who did not, such as the Chinese in China and Hong Kong, the Malayans, and the Filipinos, who were anticipating their independence from the United States in another few months.

Two weeks after the beginning of the war (December 1941), the Japanese launched a war-bond campaign, and although the Japanese people were heavily taxed and had been pressured before for more of their savings, they responded nobly.

By Christmastime the Japanese were in Borneo and fighting on Luzon, and the Japanese people learned of the great victory at Wake Island. (They did not learn of the great defeat at Wake Island, which had sent the original Japanese invading fleet scurrying back to its base for reinforcements against a handful of American aircraft and guns manned by determined but unassisted marines. They did not learn that the Japanese easy conquest of Luzon had been planned by General MacArthur so that he could concentrate his defenses on Bataan.) The Japanese victories were acclaimed as victories of Japanese power, never as strategic withdrawals by the West.

The euphoria was epidemic. In China, with no valid reason for it, the Japanese launched a Christmas offensive in Kiangsi and Hunan provinces. As always, the Japanese advanced swiftly and "crushed" the enemy. True, but the enemy picked themselves up after they had been crushed and moved away to fight again. After a few weeks in Kiangsi and Hunan, the Japanese controlled the cities, but the Chinese controlled the villages and the roads. Only in armed convoy were the Japanese safe to travel about. They had their victories, of course, but China continued to struggle on, to resist Japanese control.

News began to trickle out to the world about Japanese atrocities in Malaya, Singapore, Hong Kong, and the Philippines. Not a word of these incidents was ever to appear in the Japanese media. But to forestall any possible negative effects of accidental disclosure, the Japanese began a counterpropaganda campaign, accusing the Allies of atrocities. The British, they charged, had sent the Indian troops to the front in Hong Kong and Malaya to be massacred while the British and the Australians lolled in their country clubs. General Tojo himself, in a speech to the Diet, claimed that on Mindanao Island in the Philippines, conquering Japanese heroes had saved hundreds, thousands of Japanese from a terrible fate at the hands of the Americans. The Americans, he asserted, had tortured to death 10 Japanese civilians at the outbreak of war and had machine-gunned another 38 to death.

By Christmas, too, the Japanese could claim that they had captured North Borneo and with it, the immense petroleum resources they coveted. The navy could breathe a sigh of relief, and so could the army and navy air forces, for Japan now had the petroleum resources to fight her war in China.

What Admiral Yamamoto referred to privately as "the mindless rejoicing" continued, promoted by the government.

Some care had to be taken with the propaganda. The Germans and Italians were, after all, Japan's allies. So the propaganda had to differentiate between the "good white guys" and the "bad white guys," the latter being the "Anglo-Saxons." The Japanese were careful to gloss over the racial relationship between Anglo-Saxons and Germans.

By March 1942, when all but a handful of ragged American survivors of the Philippine campaign had been put down, Bataan was staggering, and Corregidor was getting ready to receive the full brunt of Japanese power, the Japanese government was planning its defensive posture. The admirals wanted to chew up Australia, New Zealand, and the South Pacific islands. The generals wanted to take India away from the British, and some of them dreamed of meeting Adolf Hitler's forces in the Caucasus and splitting up the world with him. General Tojo realistically hoped for less. All he wanted was to resolve the China incident so that Japan could stop bankrupting herself, financially and physically, by pouring billions of yen into the China sinkhole. For Tojo, by this time, perceived that China had become a quicksand that endangered Japan's future, yet he dared not back away from his stated position. The Japanese people had been told too many lies for too long about China to believe the truth at that point.

It was at this point that the Greater East Asia Coprosperity Sphere was conceived by Tojo as the solution to the problems of the welfare and defense of the new empire. The Europeans and Americans had all but been expelled from Asia, as promised. Now Japanese industry was to move into the newly won territories and start industries that would bring profits back to Japan and supply all her needs. The great rice bowl of Indochina, Thailand, and Burma was to be exploited to the fullest.

When all the Asian states had been made into useful parts of the new empire, the Japanese would then be able to deal with their old enemies. Perhaps Hitler would by that time have defeated them all in the West. Britain and America, obviously, would forever be forbidden from the Pacific. Perhaps Hawaii would be brought into the Japanese empire—its population was more than 30 percent Japanese—and certainly all the minor islands of the Pacific would qualify to become part of the great sea chain of Greater Nippon.

The second phase of Japan's expansion operations—the capture of the Indies and Burma—had been virtually completed by March. And what was to be the third phase?

The planners were a little fuzzy on this point; they had not expected the Japanese expansion to be so quick or so complete. India was on the agenda, and so was Australia.

But before India could be taken, an overland transport route had to be built, and that meant a Bangkok-Rangoon railroad, for which war prisoners taken on Malaya were to be used. It would take five years, said the army engineers. The distance was 400 kilometers, and most of the terrain was deep jungle over mountains and ravines.

Impossible! The job would be completed in 18 months, no more, Imperial General Headquarters told Field Marshal Terauchi, the commander of the armies in the south. The cost—which meant the lives of the prisoners of war—was unimportant. Marshal Terauchi had 16,000 prisoners of war and an unlimited supply of Chinese and Malay labor in Malaya. Let him use them.

As for Australia, it would have to await the capture of the lower Solomon Islands and New Guinea and then the Japanese occupation of the other European South Pacific islands. The landing of Japanese troops at Lae and Salamaua was the first step. They were to be joined by troops who would capture Port Moresby, an operation slated for May 1942.

By April of 1942, the truth about the circumstances surrounding the Japanese victories and occupation of Hong Kong, Singapore, Malaya, and the East Indies was beginning to filter through to the world outside the Japanese sphere of influence. Here and there a prisoner of war escaped to the West to tell his grisly tale of rape, torture, and murder at the hands of the Japanese army. These tales upset the Japanese and triggered a spate of counterpropaganda. In Shanghai, in Manila, in Hong Kong, the Japanese produced prisoners for newspaper interviews and radio broadcasts denying these accusations aimed primarily at the home audience, lest they be disillusioned, but also at the West.

This tactic did not always work. Two American officers captured at Shanghai were brought before the microphones to tell the world how well the Japanese treated their prisoners of war. Somber and restrained, they instead conveyed the message that life in Japanese captivity was no picnic. That was obviously not the story the Japanese wanted to air. They tried other POWs, and some did parrot the proper phrases about good treatment. But others were clever and subtle enough to get the real message across without openly denying the Japanese propaganda:

LIEUTENANT: I lost my bicycle when the Japanese captured me at Guam. I miss it.

NURSE: We are enjoying life immensely.

LIEUTENANT: I wish to enjoy the Japanese scenery.

NAVY COMMANDER: We are allowed to use the clothes we had on at the time of capture.

The Japanese, not understanding the Western sense of humor, did not see the anomalies in these apparently positive statements about life as a Japanese captive.

In Tokyo the euphoria of victory was virtually untouched even by these little clouds. On February 23, Imperial Headquarters told the Tokyo press about the great victory by Admiral Nagumo in the raid on Darwin; the next day it said nothing about Admiral William F. Halsey's raid on Wake Island. That news did not come out for many weeks, and when it was announced in Japan it stated that the Americans had come in with an aircraft carrier, two cruisers, and six destroyers but that the Japanese sank one cruiser, damaged a destroyer, and destroyed five enemy planes, with only negligible damage to Japanese installations. The Americans were just beginning to learn about offensive naval action. The Halsey raid was certainly anything but a prime success, but the Americans actually suffered little, if any, damage or losses. The carrier *Enterprise,* the two cruisers, and the destroyers did attack. The surface ships shelled Wake installations for two hours, but they were standing out 10 miles from shore, to be outside the range of Japanese shore batteries and the results were not impressive. The American guns destroyed a few buildings and sank a patrol craft in the harbor, but that was all. Next day the carrier launched an attack force of 42 planes, but all they destroyed were three flying boats in the harbor.

The raid would not have been worth the effort except that it was an offensive action, the first conducted by the Americans. The next raid was against Marcus Island, 1,000 miles southeast of Tokyo. There Halsey did even less damage and lost one aircraft.

These raids were essentially ignored by the Japanese, because they were relatively unimportant. As one American officer put it ruefully, the Japanese did not mind them any more than a dog minds a flea. In three months the Japanese forces had captured a vast new empire, suffering limited losses. The heady atmosphere of total victory and self-satisfaction had spread across all Japan.

EIGHTEEN

The Americans Strike Back

While the people of Japan were basking in the reflected glory of their military forces and congratulating one another on victory after victory, the Americans were doing what they could to restore a badly shaken home morale. Admiral Nimitz arrived at Pearl Harbor at Christmas, 1941. After surveying the scene and expressing his wonderment at Admiral Nagumo's failure to complete the job of destruction when he had that golden opportunity on December 7, Admiral Nimitz ordered Rear Admiral Herbert F. Leary and Task Force 17, built around the carrier *Saratoga*, to sea and seek out the enemy. Nimitz wanted a naval victory.

Admiral King fully expected the Japanese to continue their drive south and to make an attack on Australia and the South Pacific islands. To get ready he ordered the First Marine Division to Samoa to reinforce the American garrison there while the marines trained for action. Four transports loaded the marines at San Diego, and they started across the Pacific, escorted by Vice Admiral William F. Halsey's *Enterprise* task force and joined later by Vice Admiral Frank Jack Fletcher's *Yorktown*. Thus by January there were three American carriers in the Pacific. That worried Admiral Yamamoto, who had a much clearer view of the American potential in the war than most of his countrymen. But just then the American hopes received a setback; a Japanese submarine encountered the *Saratoga* off Midway Island and put a torpedo into her. The explosion killed six men and flooded three of the ship's fire rooms, but she did not sink. Slowly she steamed back to Pearl Harbor and then to the West Coast of the United States for drydock and repair.

Nimitz then ordered Vice Admiral Wilson Brown in the carrier *Lexington* to attack Wake Island. Brown headed that way with his carrier, several cruisers and destroyers, and the tanker *Neches*. But he got only about 150 miles west of Hawaii when the *Neches* was torpedoed by another Japanese submarine, and he had to turn around because she was the only tanker he had with him.

Admiral King was not happy. His carrier admirals had so far shown a dismal lack of aggressiveness in the war. At the beginning even Halsey had suggested that he go back to the West Coast and pick up a carrier load of aircraft to replace the planes destroyed by the Japanese at Pearl Harbor. That was defensive, not offensive, thinking, and King wanted men in charge of the Pacific navy who would think offensive action. In his mind, during the next few months the American admirals in the Pacific were all on trial.

The first to go was Admiral Leary. He was assigned to shore duty, where his long experience would be useful and he wouldn't be required to make any command decisions about combat.

Nimitz then ordered Admiral Halsey and Admiral Fletcher to speed to Samoa, unload the marines, and then move out to make a strike against the Japanese. The first target for Halsey would be the Marshall Islands, British possessions consisting of several small atolls. The Japanese had occupied the Marshalls at the beginning of the war and were turning the island group into a major central Pacific air and naval base. Halsey was assigned to strike the northern Marshalls, while Fletcher would come up from the south and hit the southern atolls. Meanwhile, Rear Admiral Raymond Spruance would take a cruiser force to Wotje Island to bombard the airfields there.

Halsey's first raid was on Roi-Namur, two atolls connected by a causeway, and Kwajalein. Before dawn on February 1 the raid began with nine torpedo planes and 37 dive bombers. They returned to announce the sinking of several Japanese ships and the destruction of many aircraft on the ground. Other planes took off and repeated the mission. For nine hours Admiral Halsey remained in the area. The Japanese counterattacked from the air, and the cruiser *Chester* was bombed by eight twin-engined level bombers. Most of the bombs fell wide, but one struck the cruiser, killing 8 men and wounding 11. After this attack Halsey knew the Japanese would return with aircraft from all the islands in the chain, so it was time to move. The American planes were called back to the carrier, and soon the carrier task force was gathering speed. It was none too soon. The Japanese had been completely alerted and knew the position of the task force. More Japanese air attacks began, and the antiaircraft gunners aboard the American ships were kept busy tracking and firing at attacking planes. One twin-engined bomber made a run on the *Enterprise,* but the bombs missed and the plane was badly damaged. The Americans then had their first taste of the Japanese spirit of Bushido, the renovated code of the samurai warriors, which told the Japanese soldier to be ready to die for emperor and country at any time. The bomber pilot, unable to sink the carrier with his bombs, decided to crash his damaged plane into the ship and came zooming down. From the bridge the captain ordered the ship turned hard to the right. On the flight deck a mechanic jumped into the rear seat of a torpedo plane, swung its machine gun around, and began firing at the Japanese bomber. Every antiaircraft gun in the fleet within range was turned on the plane.

On the bridge everybody ducked; then nearly all those present fell on top of Admiral Halsey to protect him. He picked himself up and grinned. This was action—this was what he liked.

It was not what Vice Admiral Fletcher liked. His attack on the south had not been nearly so successful as Halsey's, and he had lost six planes. He stayed less than nine hours on station, then scurried back to base, thankful he had not lost his carrier.

When Halsey returned to Pearl Harbor, his men hit the bars of Honolulu, bragging about their exploits. Their commander's reputation in the fleet was made; there was no question about his aggressiveness, either among the men or among the brass. Admiral King awarded Halsey the Distinguished Service Medal. Admiral Nimitz held a press conference, and the newspaper reporters had a field day. For a change the navy had something positive to report, something to counteract the grim news from the Philippines and the Dutch East Indies.

Admiral Halsey was soon back at sea, this time making an attack on Wake Island on February 24, 1942. Vice Admiral Brown was given a second chance to prove his mettle. Nimitz told him to go down to the South Pacific and work over the Japanese, who had just established their big army and navy base at Rabaul on New Britain Island in New Guinea and had just moved troops into Lae and Salamaua there. It was apparent to admirals King and Nimitz that the enemy was preparing for a further move to menace British New Guinea and Australia.

Off the Solomons the American carrier pilots became involved in a big air battle. Lieutenant Edward (Butch) O'Hare became an ace that day, shooting down five Japanese planes. The attack on Rabaul was successful, but Admiral Brown called it off after the one strike because he was afraid that by losing the element of surprise he was risking his carrier. His thinking reflected the peacetime doctrine of carrier warfare in the American navy: the welfare of the carrier came first; it was a precious and delicate instrument that must not be sacrificed. But what the American navy was now learning was that carriers must be put at risk if any positive results were to be obtained. Halsey saw this fact clearly and began to rely on speed and alertness to protect his carriers. But most of the other carrier admirals who had come up through the ranks during the peacetime still held those early views. Also, they were not aviators (Halsey was a pilot, although not a very good one), and they worried excessively about the dangers of air attack, too often ignoring opportunities. So Vice Admiral Brown, with plenty of targets still left, pulled his carrier force away from Rabaul, and headed back for safety.

Meanwhile, Admiral Halsey was heading for Marcus Island and another bold raid on Japanese shipping and airfields. By the time he got back to Pearl Harbor, Admiral Brown and Admiral Fletcher were out again. Admiral Brown had a suggestion for Admiral Nimitz: he would feel much more secure if the carriers operated in pairs instead of singly. That would double the number of planes available for attack, make flying combat air patrol and antisubmarine patrol more productive, and double the number of antiaircraft guns available in case of attack. Nimitz accepted the idea, and so Brown's *Lexington* and Fletcher's *Yorktown* went back to the South Pacific, where they caught a Japanese convoy at Lae. The two carriers sent a strike force of 104 aircraft against the convoy. The American planes appeared in the harbor suddenly after having cleared the mountains and completely surprised the Japanese. The Americans sank three Japanese transports, which cost the enemy the supplies and equipment for a division of troops. It was the most successful of all the raids because it stopped the Japanese advance into Lae and Salamaua.

NINETEEN

Trincomalee

Early in March 1942, Admiral Yamamoto sent Admiral Nagumo and the carrier striking force to the South Pacific to help in the new campaign to extend the Japanese empire further than anyone had expected six months earlier. Where was Japan going now? Some in Tokyo still looked longingly toward the north. In Berlin, Hitler's foreign office kept pressing the Japanese ambassador for action against the Soviet Union, since Hitler had started his war against Russia in the summer of 1941. But the Japanese generals remembered Nomonhon and the huge losses they had suffered there when they took on the Red Army. A strike north would have to wait.

So Japan had to consider the areas in which she could move. One was south, to the islands north of Australia, with an eye to attacking Australia in the future, but at the moment, the aim was to cut off Australia from America. Japan could also move east into the central Pacific area, thus strengthening her perimeter and pushing the United States back. Or she could move into the Indian Ocean and perhaps overland to the Middle East oil fields.

Raids on Darwin and Port Arthur proved effective and emphasized the power of Japan. They had set up the Java invasion and weakened the northern coast of Australia for the movement into New Guinea that was already in motion.

Admiral Yamamoto was nagged by the nightmare that had bothered him since December 8, 1941: the failure of Admiral Nagumo to destroy the power of the U.S. Pacific Fleet. Added to that was his concern about the might of the British Asiatic Fleet, which was still in the Indian Ocean. As long as these two elements remained, Japanese sea power was threatened, and sea power was the key to her expansion into the Pacific. In mid-March, Yamamoto looked ahead at possible dangers. The American carriers that Nagumo had missed at Pearl Harbor were now becoming more than a little troublesome. The U.S. raids—Kwajalein and Roi-Namur on February 1; Wake Island on February 24; Marcus Island on March 4; Rabaul on February 17; and New Guinea on March 17—were beginning to pose a real threat. Further, Yamamoto was concerned about the American ability to launch air raids on Japan from the Aleutian Islands. The Americans had the B-17 bomber, and it was no secret that they were building an even bigger, longer-range aircraft, the B-29, which the American air generals had already admitted was being developed for the bombing of Japan.

Out of this thinking and from discussions with his staff officers came Yamamoto's plans for the future operations of the Combined Fleet and its carrier striking force. To enable the Japanese to attack India, the British naval presence in the Indian Ocean had to be destroyed. For Japan to be defended against air attack by the Americans, the Aleutian Islands had to be neutralized. To ensure the safety of the inner Empire of Japan, the American carrier force had to be destroyed.

By March 1942, the British had one light carrier (*Hermes*) and two fleet carriers in the Indian Ocean, plus five battleships, seven cruisers, 16 destroyers, and seven submarines. Admiral Yamamoto decided they must be destroyed.

The first Japanese move was to occupy the Andaman Islands on March 23, 1942. These islands might become a British base for operations against Singapore. The Japanese then took Pakhet and Mergui islands, and on April 2 moved the Eighteenth Infantry Division from Singapore to Rangoon. This took 46 transports.

While the army was establishing this force for future operations against India, the navy was getting ready to clear the Indian Ocean. On March 26, Admiral Nagumo left Kendari with orders to strike at the British naval forces, which were based at Trincomalee and Colombo in Ceylon. Nagumo had the five fleet carriers *Akagi, Hiryu, Soryu, Shokaku,* and *Zuikaku,* four battleships, two cruisers, and 10 destroyers.

At the same time, two other naval forces left Japanese waters to help clear the Indian Ocean. One was a carrier strike force under Admiral Ozawa in the carrier *Ryujo.* He had five heavy cruisers, one light cruiser, and four destroyers. And—something unique for the Japanese—they sent out a submarine force to prey on merchant shipping. At and after the Pearl Harbor attack the Japanese had made no particular effort to isolate Hawaii or to attack merchant shipping, for reasons the Americans never understood. This foray into the Indian Ocean represented the first and only effort of the Japanese to destroy merchant shipping and for some reason was never repeated.

Ceylon was the last remaining Allied naval base in Asia now that Singapore had fallen, Manila was gone, and Java had been swallowed up. If the British Asiatic Fleet could be wiped out, there would be no naval force in the Pacific that could challenge Japan.

The British fleet was built around three carriers (although the Japanese knew of only one of them, the *Hermes*). The other two carriers and part of the cruiser and destroyer forces were based secretly in several obscure islands in the Indian Ocean.

The British knew the Japanese were going to attack, and on March 31 Admiral James Somerville ordered Colombo harbor cleared of ships, which were to move to Addu Atoll in the Maldive Islands, the secret British base that Japanese submarines had still not discovered, although they were operating in the area.

Admiral Nagumo's orders were to hit the British fleet, on Sunday, April 5, just as he had hit the American fleet at Pearl Harbor. Yamamoto hoped to catch the British napping as he had caught the Americans. Nagumo was warned that the fleet might be either at Colombo or Trincomalee. If he missed on April 5, he was to try the following Sunday, which was Easter and thus seemed even more promising. And, Yamamoto reminded Admiral Nagumo, whether they found the fleet or not, they were to attack port facilities and merchant shipping and were not to make the errors they had made at Pearl Harbor on December 7 but were to destroy the British ability to make war from Ceylon.

When Admiral Somerville learned the Japanese fleet was on the way, he brought his ships out of their secret base to face the enemy. He knew he couldn't outgun the Japanese in the air. His hope was to force a surface engagement in which his ships would have superior firepower. So he skirted around the enemy edges, trying to find an opening.

The Japanese hit Colombo on the morning of April 5. They found 34 merchant ships and warships in the harbor— the British had not been as careful about clearing out as they should have been, given the orders they had. The Japanese carrier planes sank a destroyer and an armed merchant cruiser and damaged a submarine tender and a merchant ship. They were careful, too, to pay attention to the workshops and shore installations and caused considerable damage to them. Late that afternoon Japanese scout bombers located the cruisers *Cornwall* and *Dorsetshire* about 200 miles south of Ceylon. Although the bombers sank both ships in about half an hour, Admiral Nagumo didn't recognize the significance of the location of the ships. In fact, they were moving toward Colombo and a rendezvous with the rest of the British fleet when they were attacked.

Thus Nagumo missed the main body of the British fleet and turned toward the east of Ceylon. He maneuvered randomly for several days and then turned back to Trincomalee on April 9. There were some service ships in port at the naval base, which Nagumo's force sank or damaged, and the harbor installations were worked over. Outside the harbor the Japanese found the old carrier *Hermes,* whose planes had been flown off, and sank her. They also sank her escorting destroyer, along with a corvette, a service ship, and a merchant ship that were found in the waters off Trincomalee.

While the carrier task force was rampaging around Ceylon, Admiral Ozawa's smaller carrier, surface force, and submarines sank 23 merchant ships, most of them on April 6, and paralyzed coastal shipping in the Bay of Bengal, which was absolutely essential for the conduct of normal life in India. The planes also attacked Cocanada and Vizagapatam.

The defeat was complete. The British, realizing they could not defend their naval forces against such Japanese might, withdrew their Eastern Fleet to Kilindi in East Africa. The Japanese now ruled all Asian waters, although once again, Admiral Yamamoto was displeased because Admiral Nagumo had failed to conduct a clean sweep and two British fleet carriers had escaped.

TWENTY

Air Raid on Tokyo!

At the beginning of the Pacific war General Tojo and his military men had promised the people of Japan they would never be bombed the way the British had been by the Germans. By March 1942, the possibility of such a bombing seemed to exist only in the future, and, if it came at all, would come from the Aleutian Islands. Admiral Yamamoto was preparing to take care of that possibility with a naval operation that would neutralize the Aleutians for good. So the Japanese people remained complacent with their string of victories.

Across the Pacific, the Americans were anything but complacent. To be sure, in March the "Battling Bastards of Bataan" were still holding out and the fortress of Corregidor was still in American hands. But in Washington the nation's leaders knew it was only a matter of time before the American presence in the Philippines would be only a memory. President Roosevelt had ordered General MacArthur out of the islands to reconstitute the war effort in Australia. The president and his chief military officers knew it was going to be a long way back to Manila. So many defeats had kept American morale at a very low ebb, but there was not much action that could be taken at the moment, because the president had been persuaded by Prime Minister Churchill that the major American war effort had to be aimed at Hitler in Europe instead of Tojo in Japan.

Since nothing could be done to save the Philippines and since it was too early to expect General MacArthur to produce any action, and while the U.S. Navy was in the process of rebuilding and repairing the ravages of Pearl Harbor, any boost to American morale in the Pacific had to be spectacular but not expensive in terms of men and material.

What could be done?

Bomb Tokyo! somebody said.

And so a plan was born.

General H. H. Arnold, chief of the Army air forces, and Admiral King received the plan and liked it. It could be carried out with relatively little risk: it would involve one or two aircraft carriers, transporting a squadron of army medium bombers. Why army bombers? Because the navy had no medium bombers, and carrier bombers had far too short a range (about 350 miles) for such a job. To move to within 350 miles of the Japanese islands would be to endanger the carrier and make it almost a certainty it would be attacked and perhaps sunk. The carrier would have to launch its planes from much farther away than that, outside the range of Japanese land-based aircraft, and so the medium bomber was the weapon needed. But, if they sent medium bombers over Japan, planes would be unable to get back to the carrier, because the carrier could not wait for them. So the bombers would have to land somewhere else. The only place they could land was in China, where although the Japanese held the coastlines and most of the cities, the Chinese held huge sectors of the interior, including a number of airfields. It was quite conceivable that the medium bombers could land safely in China, and even if they did not and the crews had to parachute, they would be among friendly people, allies.

General Arnold and Admiral King took their idea to President Roosevelt, who liked it, as they were sure he would. It had a spectacular element to it, something that always appealed to Roosevelt.

So the plan was born in February, while Admiral Halsey was out making his strikes against the Japanese bases at Wake Island, the Marshall Islands, and Marcus Island. One afternoon in March 1942, Admiral Halsey returned to Pearl Harbor and walked into Admiral Nimitz's headquarters to report. He found Nimitz talking to Captain Donald W. Duncan, who had brought the plan for an air attack on Tokyo to Pearl Harbor. That day Nimitz, Halsey, and Duncan agreed the plan was possible, and Halsey was eager to carry it out. But when the matter was discussed with Nimitz's staff, the conservative Admiral Milo Draemel, Nimitz's chief of staff, expressed his opinion that the raid was a foolish and wasteful stunt. Probably all the planes would be lost, he said. Probably so would many of the crews. They would certainly be better expended somewhere else fighting the enemy rather than pulling a stunt.

Admiral Nimitz admitted cheerfully that everything Admiral Draemel said was true, but that what Draemel was unaware of (and the reason he was soon shipped off to the mainland to run a navy yard instead of a navy) was the morale factor. American morale desperately needed a boost to help the war effort, and the Tokyo raid would certainly provide it. So Draemel was overruled and the raid was on.

General Arnold had already chosen the man who would lead the Tokyo air raid. He was a feisty little retread officer from World War I, a racing pilot and test pilot who would go anywhere and do anything for excitement. He had come back into the service as a lieutenant colonel for this war, and he was itching for action. His name was James H. Doolittle.

Halsey and Doolittle met in San Francisco to talk about the raid. Halsey said he was eager to carry it out, but that Doolittle had to realize it might never come about. Doolittle was puzzled until Halsey explained that if the carrier were "spooked" (surprised), all the B-25 medium bombers on the flight deck would have to be pushed into the sea so that the aircraft carrier could launch its own planes and defend itself.

That was a shocker, but Doolittle had to accept it and hope for the best.

Back at Pearl Harbor the planners consulted with Halsey and put together a task force. It would include the carrier *Enterprise* and the new carrier *Hornet,* which would actually carry the B–25 aircraft on its decks. But it was not as simple as that; the B–25s had to be modified for the special mission and be fitted with gas tanks if they were to reach the China coast. The *Hornet* would leave Norfolk, Virginia, where she was being fitted out for sea, load the B–25s at San Francisco, and then head into the Pacific. Admiral Halsey, operating out of Pearl Harbor, would rendezvous with the *Hornet,* and the two carriers and their support ships would head for Japan.

On April 1, as the Japanese carrier force began its movements in the Indian Ocean, the *Hornet* was at the Alameda Air Station on San Francisco Bay, loading up the medium bombers. An elaborate cover story was concocted at Alameda, on the premise that the Japanese had agents everywhere in America. This belief was a hangover from the deep distrust with which Caucasian Americans regarded their Japanese-American citizens, and it was totally unjustified. There is no record of any Japanese-American before or during World War II, attempting to give any information to the Japanese enemy. But certainly other Americans talked a lot, so the concocted story served well. When the word got around San Francisco that the *Hornet* was taking planes to Hawaii for air defense, a representative of the North American Aviation Company, which had manufactured the planes, insisted he absolutely had to sail on the carrier to Oahu where he had important business with the army. The civilian was insistent and threatened to go straight to Washington if he was refused. Captain Marc Mitscher tried to dissuade him with all sorts of arguments, but the civilian was obdurate, and finally Captain Mitscher shrugged and told him to come along if he insisted.

So, triumphant, the manufacturers' agent came aboard. The loading was finished, the crew had all returned to the ship, and on April 2 she sailed. Just inside the Golden Gate she picked up the cruiser *Vincennes,* the light cruiser *Nashville,* the oiler *Cimarron,* and four destroyers. That afternoon, as the aircraft company's agent basked in the sun, enjoying the sea breeze and congratulating himself on getting his transportation to Hawaii, Captain Mitscher announced on the ship's loudspeaker system that they were not going to Hawaii but to Japan. It would be several weeks before North American's agent saw Pearl Harbor.

Captain Mitscher then told the crew they were going to approach Japan and launch the 16 B–25s for a raid on Tokyo. The crew rose up cheering, and that day one of them composed a victory song to be sung to the tune of the marching song of the Seven Dwarfs in the current Walt Disney cartoon feature *Snow White.*

The weather turned rough and the army mechanics watched over their aircraft like nursemaids, tinkering with this part and that to make sure everything would be ready to go at the appointed hour. Jimmy Doolittle briefed his men and briefed them again. All of them had trained in simulated carrier takeoffs from a short runway, and they knew they could do it. Landing was something else, but it was not something they could worry about at that point. Their fate would depend on the wind and weather over China after they had finished their bombing raid.

The crews studied maps and their various targets. They would hit not just Tokyo but also Yokohama, Nagoya, and Osaka. Industrial Japan would have a taste of what bombing was like. They were coached by the carrier's air intelligence officer, who had spent some time in the U.S. naval attache's office in Tokyo. Doolittle wanted a night takeoff if possible, about three hours before dawn. That would allow them to catch the Japanese early in the morning and then head for the China coast, arriving at the Chinese bases before dark if they were lucky. If they were not discovered earlier by the Japanese, the mission was to be carried out on April 19.

Admiral Halsey's task force left Pearl Harbor on the

morning of April 8 with two more cruisers, three destroyers, and two tankers. The two task forces headed for their rendezvous point.

On April 9 the force at sea got the bad news that General King had surrendered Bataan to the Japanese, although General Wainwright was still holding out on Corregidor. More than ever the American people needed something to lift their spirits and counteract the air of defeat that seemed to be everywhere in the Pacific.

On April 16 the carrier task forces had a shock; Radio Tokyo announced that someone had claimed to have bombed Tokyo and that this was impossible. No planes could come within 500 miles of Tokyo, the Japanese boasted. That day the task forces made their rendezvous and steamed on toward Japan. They refuelled at sea, and on the night of April 17 Admiral Halsey passed the word from the *Enterprise* to Doolittle that they were moving in fast. The carriers would run at high speed all night and then the next day until they either reached the agreed launch point or were discovered.

The radar crew of the task force were alert that night, and just after three o'clock in the morning they saw two blips on their radarscopes, blips that represented Japanese picket vessels. The Japanese had established a broad picket line around their islands to prevent enemy ships from getting through. The carrier force changed course abruptly, swinging 90 degrees to starboard to get away from the picket ships, and the task force came to general quarters. Both forces steamed away from the blips for an hour before turning back to the base course.

But shortly after dawn, one of the morning air patrol planes from the *Enterprise* spotted a Japanese patrol craft on his search pattern. He reported back to Admiral Halsey that he had seen the ship change course and men pointing up at him, so he had obviously been discovered. Halsey had to assume the patrol craft had reported the presence of enemy carrier planes (he was quite right; the report had gone out immediately).

Just then the radio operators on the American ships heard

messages being sent, and another American patrol plane spotted another Japanese coastal patrol ship. Halsey ordered the cruiser *Vincennes* to sink the Japanese vessel, but he knew that he must now make his move. They were 625 miles off the Japanese coast. Doolittle had been hoping he could be brought to within 500 miles of Japan, but that was now impossible. The extra distance meant an increase in the odds, but the choices were clear: either take the chance or scrub the whole operation and push the bombers over the side. No one wanted to do that, so Doolittle gave the order, and at 8 o'clock that morning the B–25s began taking off and winging their way toward Tokyo and their other targets.

All the planes got off, and all got to Japan. Doolittle hit Tokyo with fire bombs just after noon, and all the other planes also hit their targets. Not one was shot down by antiaircraft fire. But after they left Japan their luck changed. Those extra hundred miles made a lot of difference. Not one of the B–25s made it to a Chinese airfield. They ditched either off the China coast or on the beach, or the crews bailed out.

The next day Radio Tokyo was buzzing with the (for them) devastating news. President Roosevelt announced to the American public that American planes had bombed To-kyo, a message that electrified the American people. The news did everything for American morale that Admiral King and General Arnold had hoped, and it confused the Japa-nese. The president announced that the planes had taken off from a base called Shangri-la (a mystical place in a movie about a Tibetan hideaway of that name was popular just then). The Japanese knew the planes had come from a carrier and were very upset that a carrier had managed to come in so close without detection. Further, General Tojo and the navy had both lost face because they had promised the Japanese people they would never be bombed. So the Jap-anese erupted in fury. One of the people who had opposed the Doolittle Tokyo raid was Generalissimo Chiang Kai-shek of the Republic of China. When apprised of the plan, he had said it would probably cost him a half million lives.

He knew his Japanese, and he knew that if the Japanese homeland was bombed and the planes headed for China, the Japanese would take out their anger on his people.

Chiang was quite right. General Tojo immediately ordered a campaign in central China to capture all the airfields for which the Doolittle fliers were to head, thus making sure that never again would an Allied airplane be able to use a Chinese airfield against Japan. The Japanese soldiers were ruthless as they marched through the Chinese countryside, particularly when they discovered some villages that had helped Doolittle fliers after they landed. The men and boys of these villages were killed; in some cases all the people were murdered. More than a quarter of a million Chinese were killed in the aftermath of the Tokyo bombing.

Most of the B-25 crews managed to parachute to safety or to get out of their ditched or crash-landed aircraft. Some were wounded. The crews of two of the B-25s were captured, and three crew members were tried for ''war crimes'' and their heads cut off by the Japanese. Five other Americans were held in prison camps; one of them starved to death.

Admiral Halsey and his two-carrier task force turned around after launching the planes and headed back for Pearl Harbor. On their way home they passed not too far from Admiral Nagumo's Japanese Carrier Strike Force, but the enemies did not meet—not that time.

TWENTY-ONE

High Tide

On April 14, 1942, Tokyo was again exultant.

BATAAN FALLS, said the big headlines in all the capital city's newspapers. CORREGIDOR COLLAPSE IMMINENT.

But the collapse of the last bastion of American defense in the Philippines was not quite imminent, despite the Japanese yearning for the clean sweep of the Pacific for which they had waited these last six weeks. Imperial General Headquarters had become spoiled by success and impatient with delay. General Honma was virtually in disgrace already, although he had succeeded in his enterprise. But he had not succeeded quickly enough, and the ragged remnants of American power, clustered in the caves and tunnels of Corregidor, were an embarrassment to the victors of the Pacific.

The holdouts on Corregidor deserved no praise, said General Takaaki Kuwaki. Any army, he claimed, could have held out for weeks in the rugged terrain of Bataan.

The Japanese newspaper photographers were having a field day with the former American presence; a Japanese flag waved belligerently above the sign "U.S. Navy Base, Mariveles." And every day the newspapers reported that Japanese artillery was "smashing the enemy" on the rock of Corregidor. The fortress was at the edge of defeat under the "furious onslaughts" of the Japanese. It was true the onslaughts were furious; all day bombs rained down and all day artillery thundered at Corregidor. But the island held out and, along with the Doolittle bombing of Tokyo, continued to be an embarrassment to the Japanese. This was part of the reason for the fury expended on the Doolittle fliers when a few of them were captured.

On the night of May 5 the Japanese decided it was time to put an end to the opposition on Corregidor, and they moved in at least 300 field pieces. A sheet of smoke and flame settled over the fortress. As the shells ate away at the rock, landslides swept down the steep slopes and hid the beach from view.

After hours of the barrage, a green rocket finally flared, and the Japanese began coming across in small boats to "The Rock," landing on the north shore. The American machine guns of Melinta Hill began to fire on the invaders, but on they came for awhile. Finally the Japanese troop commander decided the hill was not yet ready, so the troops moved back and the barrage began again. It lasted another hour; then Melinta Hill was still as the Japanese attacked.

The attack quieted down but began again at about 5 A.M., this time concentrated on Monkey Point. With the light of day the Japanese dive bombers and level bombers came over, hitting Corregidor and Fort Hughes again and again.

At 10:30 that morning the American order came to scuttle all ships and boats in the harbor, and those aboard the ships saw white flags going up on Corregidor. But the Japanese were merciless; they kept right on firing. The men at Fort Hughes spiked their guns and raised the white flag of surrender. Soon the whole fortress was quiet. General Wainwright, with Japanese on every side and nowhere to go, finally had to surrender.

So the Japanese drive south into the Pacific had hit its high-water mark. They had captured all the territory they had set out to take. Now they had to make final some new plans that were coming through. The Japanese army had decided to move in force against British New Guinea. The navy had decided to gain a foothold in the Aleutian Islands, capture Midway, and proceed at leisure against Hawaii, while in the South Pacific they planned to cut Australia's sea line to America, preparatory to an invasion of the Australian continent.

General Douglas MacArthur had hurried to Australia on his president's orders, prepared to launch countermoves against the Japanese, but when he got there he found no troops and no equipment with which to work. Any offensive action seemed months in the future. It was true that the submarines of the Asiatic Fleet had mostly escaped and had made new bases in Australia, but submarines, no matter how effective, could not hold or capture territory.

So as of the first of May 1942, the Japanese, looking around them, could not help but be ebullient. The China campaign seemed to have gained new life, while in the south, Rabaul was being extended as the major advance base for the next big Japanese jump in the South Pacific. There seemed to be nothing in the world that could stop them.

BIBLIOGRAPHICAL NOTES

The research for this book was done largely in Tokyo at the Japanese Defense Agency's War History Room. I also used the files of *The Japan Times*, *Asahi Shimbun*, and *Mainichi Shimbun*, which were the most important newspapers of the day.

1 Preparations

The material about the Mukden incident of 1931 comes from several books, the most detailed of which are Liang Chin-tung's *The Sinister Face Of The Mukden Incident*, published by St. John's University Press in New York, 1969, and Yoshihashi Takehiko's *Conspiracy At Mukden*, published by Yale University Press, 1963.

Other material for this chapter comes from the same research sources I used in my *Japan's War*.

2 Psychology of War

Much of the material for this chapter comes from the accounts of the official Imperial Conferences. The best book to describe what happened in 1941 is Ike Nobutaka's *Japan's Decision For War: The Records of the 1941 Policy Conferences*, published by the Stanford University Press, 1967. The material about the U.S. Asiatic Fleet is from my own book on that subject, *The Lonely Ships,* published by Berkley Books, NY, 1990.

3 Pearl Harbor

The best account of the attack on Pearl Harbor is Gordon Prange's *While We Slept,* published by the McGraw-Hill Publishing Co., 1981. Those who want to pursue the Japanese motivation might look at my *Admiral Yamamoto,* also published by McGraw-Hill, 1990.

4 Grand Sweep Plan

The materials for this chapter come from many sources, assembled over a long period of time. Except for the official 101-volume Japanese war history published by the Japanese Defense Department, there is no overall picture available of the Japanese march during this six-month period.

5 The Tiger in Malaya

The account of General Yamashita's drive through Malaya can be found in the Japanese official volume on the subject, plus *Maraya,* a history of the campaign (Tokyo, 1958), and John Deane Potter's *The Life and Death of a Japanese General,* published by Signet Books/New American Library, NY, 1962.

6 Invading the Philippines

The story of the invasion of the Philippines was taken from Samuel Eliot Morison's *History of U.S. Naval Operations in World War II* and from the *U.S. Army History of the War.* My *The Lonely Ships* tells the story of the Asiatic Fleet during this period.

7 Bataan

The story of the Bataan struggles can be found in various Japanese and American official war histories and in my account of the U.S. Asiatic Fleet, *The Lonely Ships*.

8 The Fall of Singapore

The material about the fall of Singapore was taken from the Japanese official war history and from the biography of General Yamashita.

9 Striking the Indies

The account of the invasion of the Dutch East Indies is available in Samuel Eliot Morison's account of U.S. naval operations, *The Lonely Ships*, and Japanese official history volumes that deal with naval and army operations.

10 The Juggernaut Advances

The sources for this chapter are *The Lonely Ships*, Morison's history of U.S. naval operations in World War II (Little Brown, 1950–1965), and the Japanese official war history.

11 Invading Java

The story of the invasion of Java comes from the Japanese official war history, *The Lonely Ships*, and the Morison history of U.S. naval operations. I found Admiral Thomas Hart's oral history at the Navy Department library very useful.

12 The Japanese Move In

Much of the material for this chapter is available in the story of the Life and Death of the Asiatic Fleet. The *Lonely Ships* was also valuable.

13 End of the Asiatic Fleet

Again *The Lonely Ships* was valuable. So was my story of the USS *Bowfin* (Van Nostrand, 1980), a submarine of the fleet that more or less symbolizes the events of the time. Admiral Hart's oral history was also useful.

14 Conquest of Java

The official Japanese war history was primary for this chapter. The biography of General Tojo by Courtney Brown was also useful. So was my own biography of Admiral Yamamoto. The files of *Asahi* and *The Japan Times* yielded much material about reactions in Japan.

15 The Fall of Bataan

The Japanese war history, the Morison history, Donald Knox's *Death March* were all consulted here. The files of *Asahi* and *The Japan Times* were essential.

16 Death March

The official Japanese history and *Death March* were important here.

17 Japan's War

The material about reactions in Japan to the enormous success of their military forces comes from the Japanese newspapers, for the most part, as noted in their bibliographical notes.

18 The Americans Strike Back

The source for the narrative and discussion of American reactions and activities in the first days of the war is American newspapers, especially *The New York Times* and the Honolulu *Star-Bulletin,* and the records of the U.S. Pacific Fleet in Washington.

19 Trincomalee

The sources for the information about the Japanese attack in the Indian Ocean and British operations there are the Japanese official war history and the Public Records office in Kew, outside London.

20 Air Raid on Tokyo!

The source for the material on James Doolittle's raid on Tokyo is basically James Doolittle, whom I interviewed at length some years ago. Other material comes from the Pacific Fleet records.

21 High Tide

The source for this material on the Japanese reaction to the first six months of the war is the Japanese newspapers.

INDEX

Abe, Tomojo, 135
Airfield Number One, 107
Airfield Number Two, 107
Akagi, 29, 32, 172
Albacore bombers, 86
Alden, 127
Allison, John M., 12
Ambon, 100
American Asiatic Fleet: *See* U.S. Asiatic Fleet
Amur River, 10
Aparri, 59–60
Arizona, 34
Arnold, H. H., 176, 177, 181
Asagumo, 119, 122
Asaka, Prince, 7
Asashio, 111
Ashigara, 131

B–17 aircraft, 25, 60, 73, 100, 171
B–17 Flying Fortresses, 111
B–25 aircraft, 177, 178, 179, 181, 182
B–29 aircraft, 171
Bali, 110–112
Balikpapan, 93–97, 100
Banckert, 106

Bangkok-Rangoon railroad, 162
Banka Island, 104–105
Barker, 101, 106
Bataan Defense Force, 66
Bataan Peninsula, 59, 66–67, 78–83, 138–146; and American surrender at, 144–146; and evacuation of prisoners from, 147–155
Batavia, 123
Battle of Badung Strait, 110–112
Battle of the Points, 81
Bay of Bengal, 174
Benjamin Franklin, 108
Bennett, Gordon, 89
Bermingham, John L., 70–72
Betty bombers, 126
Binford, Commander, 123, 127
Bittern, 58
Blinn, W. C., 96
Boise, 93, 97, 113
Brereton, General, 114
Brett, G. H., 73, 92, 114
British Asiatic Fleet, 171, 172
British Eastern Fleet, 133

Brooke-Popham, Robert, 47, 48, 49, 73
Brown, Wilson, 166, 168, 169
Buffalo fighters, 86
Bukit Timah, 90
Bulkeley, John D., 138–139
Bulmer, 101, 106
Bushido, Japanese spirit of, 167

Calamba, 66
California, 34
Camiguin Island, 59
Camp O'Donnell, 155
Canopus, 78
Cassin, 35
Cavite, 58–59, 76, 140
Champlin, Malcolm, 76, 77, 139
Chankufeng Hill, 10
Chapple, W. G., 63
Childs, 100
China, 2–10, 159–160, 161, 182; and U.S. involvement in, 7–9
Ching-wei, Wang, 7, 9, 14
Chitose, 64
Chokai, 105
Churchill, Winston, 44, 45, 114, 175
Cimarron, 179
Clark Field, 56, 57, 63
Cocanada, 174
Collingsworth, 114
Collins, John, 68
Colombo, 173
Combined Fleet (Japan), 18
Combined Strike Force (U.S.), 101, 105, 115
Cornwall, 173
Corregidor Island, 67, 77, 78, 138–146; and American surrender at, 183–184

Danae, 116
Darwin, Australia, 108–100
De Ruyter, 101, 102, 105, 106, 111, 116, 117, 118, 119, 121, 123–124
Destroyer Division 58 (U.S.), 127
Destroyer Division 59 (U.S.), 94
Distant Cover Force (Japan), 62
Doenitz, Admiral, 61
Doolittle, James H., 177–178, 179, 180, 181
Doorman, Admiral, 101, 102–103, 104, 105, 106, 107, 108, 111, 115, 116–117, 118, 119–120, 121, 122, 123, 124
Dorsetshire, 173
Downes, 35
Draemel, Milo, 177
Dragon, 116
Duncan, Brigadier, 85
Duncan, Donald W., 177
Dutch East Indies, 67, 68, 92–98, 113
Dutch torpedo boats, 111–112

Edsall, 125, 126
Edwards, 101
Eighteenth Division (Japan), 42, 48, 49, 86, 87, 88
Electra, 115, 117, 120–121
Eleventh Air Fleet (Japan), 56, 64, 92, 101
Eleventh Division (Japan), 6
Eleventh Indian Division, 47

Eleventh Infantry Division (U.S.), 60, 78

Encounter, 115, 120, 121, 123, 127, 131

Endau River estuary, 86

Enterprise, 163, 165, 167, 178, 180

Evertsen, 128, 130

Exeter, 105, 106, 115, 116, 117, 118, 119–120, 121, 127, 131

Fife, James, 77

Fifth Air Force (U.S.), 62

Fifth Division (Japan), 42, 49, 74, 75, 82, 84, 86, 87, 88, 90

Fifty-first Infantry Division (U.S.), 66, 78, 80

Fifty-seventh Infantry Regiment (U.S.), 78, 79

Fifty-sixth Division (Japan), 42, 75

Finch, 24

First Infantry Regiment (U.S.), 67, 78

First Marine Division (U.S.), 165

First Philippine Corps, 78

Fletcher, Frank Jack, 165, 166, 168, 169

Fort Hughes, 184

Forty-eighth Infantry Division (Japan), 63, 65–66, 67, 79, 110–111

Forty-fifth Indian Brigade, 85

Forty-fifth Infantry (U.S.), 80

Forty-first Infantry Division (U.S.), 66, 78

Forty-fourth Indian Brigade, 89

14 Flying Fortresses, 62

Fourteenth Army (Japan), 65–66

Fourteenth Naval District (U.S.), 33

Fourth Marine Regiment (U.S.), 24

Fubuki, 128–129

Glassford, William A., 8, 13–14, 23, 24, 25, 59, 64, 68, 69, 73, 93, 94, 97–98, 114, 125, 127, 128, 132

Grant, E., 108

Greater East Asia Coprosperity Sphere, 158, 161

Gumbatsu, 17

Haguro, 100, 116, 117, 119, 121, 131

Halsey, William F., 163, 164, 165, 166, 167–168, 169, 177–178, 179–180, 181, 182

Hart, Thomas, 9, 12–13, 58, 59, 63, 64, 69, 72, 81, 92, 93, 97–98, 101, 102–103

Haruna, 54

Hashimoto, Rear Admiral, 105

Hayataka Maru, 63

Hayo Maru, 63

Helena, 35

Helfrich, C. E. L., 68, 113, 114, 115, 122, 124, 125, 128

Hermes, 171, 172, 174

Heron, 72–73

Hirohito, Emperor, 4, 10, 16, 17, 21–22, 23, 43

Hirota, Koki, 4

Hiryu, 100, 172

Hitler, Adolf, 28, 170

Hitokappu Wan, 30
Hobart, 105, 106, 116
Holland, 101
Honma, General, 65, 66, 79, 80, 81, 82, 138, 140, 141, 149, 183
Honolulu, 35
Hornet, 178
Hospital No. 1, 143
Hospital No. 2, 143–144
Houston, 9, 101, 102, 103, 105, 113, 115, 116, 117, 118, 119, 121, 122, 123, 124, 127, 128–130
Hudson bombers: *See* Lockheed Hudson bombers
Hull, Cordell, 8, 30
Hunan province, 159
Hurricane fighter planes, 86
Hyderabad Infantry Regiment (Indian), 49

Ikatini, Colonel, 88
Imamura, Hitoshi, 129, 132, 134, 136
Imaye, General, 91
Imperial General Headquarters, 67, 82, 132, 138, 140, 162, 163, 183
Imperial Guards Division, 75, 84, 85, 86, 87, 88, 90, 91
Indian Ocean, 172–174
Indomitable, 44–45
Ishihara, Kanji, 5
Isthmus of Kra, 41

Japanese Octopus, 104
Japanese proclamation, 140–141
Japanese victories, 156–164
Java, 64, 103, 105–112, 132

Java, 105, 106, 111, 116, 117, 118, 119, 121, 123, 124
Java Sea, 125; battle of, 114–124
Jintsu, 100, 110, 117, 120, 122
John D. Edwards, 127
John D. Ford, 94–97, 106, 111, 127
Johore, 75
Johore Strait, 86–87
Jukka Maru, 96
Jupiter, 115, 117, 120, 121, 123

Kai-shek, Chiang, 3, 6, 9, 14, 20–21, 156, 181–182
Katagiri, Eikichi, 55
Kawanishi flying boats, 70, 71, 72
Kendari Bay, 100
Kenney, George, 62
Kiangsi province, 159
Kimmel, Husband E., 29, 33
Kimura, Kaoki, 80
King, Admiral, 69, 98, 165, 166, 168, 176, 181
King, General, 144
Kirishima, 53
Koga, Mineichi, 40
Kojima, Captain, 105
Kondo, Nobutake, 62, 94, 108
Konoye, Fumimaro, 4–5, 11, 15, 16, 21, 22
Korean service troops, 151
Kortenauer, 106, 119, 123
Kota Bharu, 48–49
Kuala Lumpur, 74–75
Kumano, 105
Kureatake Maru, 96

Kurita, Admiral, 114
Kuwaki, Takaaki, 183
Kwantung army, 10, 11

Lae, 169
Langley, 13, 113, 125–127
Leary, Herbert F., 165, 166
Legaspi, 61–62
Legaspi force, 63
Lexington, 166, 169
Lingayen Gulf, 62–63
Lockheed Hudson bombers,
    71, 72, 86
Luzon, 13, 24, 140

MacArthur, Douglas, 45, 63,
    64, 65, 77, 79, 80, 139,
    159, 175, 176, 185
McCloy, R. C., 33
McConnell, R. P., 125, 126
Mainichi Shimbun (Japanese
    newspaper), 15, 17, 157
Makassar Strait, 101–102
Makassar Town, 103, 104
Malaya, 41–43, 46–52
Maldive Islands, 172–173
Manila, 75–76
Manila Bay, 143–144
Manunda, 108
Marblehead, 93, 94, 97, 101–
    102, 103, 105, 113
Marco Polo Bridge, 2
Marcus Island, 164, 169
Mariveles, 77, 78, 144
Marshall Islands, 166
Maryland, 34
Matsui, Iwane, 4, 5, 6
Matsuoka, Yosuke, 22
Meigs, 109
Meiji era, 1
Melinta Hill, 184
Michishio, 111

Midway Island, 134, 166
Mikuma, 105
Mindanao, 64
Mindanao, 59, 140
Minesweeper No. 19, 60
Minesweeper No. 10, 61
Mitscher, Marc, 178, 179
Mogami, 105
Monaghan, 35
Monkey Point, 78, 184
Morioka, Susumu, 65
Morison, Samuel Eliot, 35
Mount Samat, 141–143
Muar River, 75, 84–85
Murasame, 73
Musashio, 104
Myoko, 131, 132

Nachi, 100, 116, 117, 121,
    131
Nagano, Osami, 21, 27, 28,
    29
Nagumo, Chuichi, 29, 32,
    36, 37, 40, 108, 158, 163,
    165, 170, 171, 172, 173–
    174, 182
Naka, 96
Nakajima, Kesago, 6, 7
Nakasone, Major, 41, 42, 46
Nana Maru, 93
Nanking, 6; rape of, 7
Nara, Akira, 79
Nashville, 179
Natsushio, 103
Naval air service (Japan), 54–
    55
Naval bombers (Japan), 51–
    52
Neches, 166
Neighborhood Associations,
    157
Neosho, 35

Netherlands East Indies
   Army, 114
New Orleans, 35
Nimitz, Chester, 36, 165,
   166, 168, 169, 177
Ninety-first Division (U.S.),
   78
Ninth Infantry (Japan), 79
Nishimura, Admiral, 61, 85,
   87, 88–89, 91, 96, 115
Nojima, 73
North American Aviation
   Company, 178

Oahu, 13, 24, 140
Oglala, 35
O'Hare, Edward (Butch), 168
Oklahoma, 34
One hundred-sixteenth Infan-
   try (Japan), 65
Operation Matador, 47, 48
Oshio, 111
Otus, 103
Ozawa, Admiral, 94, 105,
   106, 107, 172, 174

P–40 fighters, 82, 109
Palembang, 104–105, 106,
   107
Palliser, Admiral, 132
Panay, 14; incident, 7
Pandan, 61
Parker, George M., 66, 78
Parrott, 94–97, 106
Patrol Wing, 10, 76
Pattani, 49
Paul Jones, 94–97, 101, 127
PBY aircraft (U.S.), 64, 70,
   72, 76, 100, 108, 109
Pearl Harbor, 26–38, 156–
   157; attack on, 34–35

Peary, 64, 69–72, 97, 108,
   109
Pecos, 131
Pennsylvania, 34
Percival, Arthur, 46, 47, 87,
   88, 89, 90
Permit, 139
Perth, 115, 116, 118, 119,
   121, 123, 124, 127, 128–
   129
Petrel, 40
Philippines, 43–45, 53–67
Phillips, Thomas, 50–51, 52
Piet Hein, 111
Pigeon, 24, 76
Pillsbury, 64, 69, 101
Plan Matador: *See* Operation
   Matador
Pope, 94–97, 106, 111, 127,
   131–132
Port Arthur, 18
Porten, General, 114
Pownall, H. R., 92
Prince of Wales, 44, 49–50,
   52
Prisoners of war: march from
   Bataan, 147–155; treatment
   of, 134–136
PT boats, 82
PT–41, 138
Purnell, Admiral, 68, 114,
   127

Queen Tunnel, 76

Rabaul, 168
Raleigh, 35
Repulse, 44, 49–50, 52
Robinson, Captain, 101, 102
Rockwell, F. W., 64, 77, 81,
   139
Roi-Namur, 167–168

Rome-Berlin-Tokyo Axis, 11–12, 15
Rooks, Captain, 128, 129, 130
Roosevelt, Franklin D., 13, 14, 21, 175, 176, 181
Roosevelt, Theodore, 2
Royal Navy, 44
Russian Far Eastern Fleet, 18
Russo-Japanese War, 2, 32
Ryujo, 44, 64, 105, 131–132, 172
Ryujo Maru, 43

S–38, 63
S–37, 103, 104
S–36, 25
Sagami Maru, 111
Sagiri, 73
St. Louis, 35
Sakai, Saburo, 53–56
Sakura Maru, 129
San Fernando Point, 63
Sangley Point, 76–77
Sanuki Maru, 63
Sanyo Maru, 61
Saratoga, 165, 166
Sasebo special landing troops (Japan), 104
Scout, 116
Seadragon, 139
Sealion, 58
Seawolf, 61, 77, 139
Second Fleet (Japan), 93–94
Second Formosan Regiment (Japan), 65
Second Indian Brigade, 90
Second Philippine Corps, 78–79
Senjinkun (pamphlet), 20
Seventy-first Infantry Division (U.S.), 66

Sewell, Colonel, 145
Shark, 64
Shaw, 35
Shokaku, 172
Singapore Island, 75, 87–91
Singora, 48, 49
Sixteenth Division (Japan), 6, 63, 65
Sixth Division (Japan), 6
Sixty-fifth Infantry Brigade (Japan), 79
Slim River, 74–75
Smuts, Jan, 45
Somerville, James, 172, 173
Soryu, 100, 172
Sosa, Tanetsuga, 134
Southern Expeditionary Force, 94
Spruance, Raymond, 167
Stark, Harold, 24
Stewart, 101, 106, 111, 113
Stimson, Henry, 144
Subic Bay, 77
Sugita, Captain, 90, 91
Sugiyama, Hajime, 4, 5, 21–22
Sukarno, Achmed, 136
Sumatra, 108
Sunda Strait, 128–130
Supreme War Council, 22, 23
Surabaya, 100, 115
Suzuya, 105

Tainan Air Flotilla, 56
Takagi, Admiral, 118, 119, 120, 122, 123, 131
Takahaski, Admiral, 94, 131
Takeda, Prince, 43
Talbot, Paul, 94, 95, 96, 97
Talomo Bay, 64
Tanaka, Raizo, 100

Tanaka detachment, 60
Tani, Hisao, 6
Task Force 5 (U.S.), 68, 69, 70
Task Force 17 (U.S.), 165
Tatsukami Maru, 96
Tenedos, 116
Tennessee, 34
Terauchi, Count, 43, 67, 75, 91, 162
Thai-Burma railroad, 133
Third Division (Japan), 42
Third Fleet (Japan), 94
Thirty-eighth Division (Japan), 40
Thirty-first Infantry Division (U.S.), 66, 80
Thirty-third Infantry (Japan), 65
Timor, 110
Togo, Heihachiro, 18
Tojo, Hideki, 4, 15, 20, 23, 28, 32, 44, 91, 132, 133, 156, 157–158, 160, 161, 175, 181, 182
Tokitsukaze, 118–119
Tokyo air raid, 176–182
Torpedoes, submarine, 61
Treaty of Portsmouth, 2
Trincomalee, 173–174
Tromp, 101, 105, 106, 111
Trout, 139
Tsuji, Lieutenant Colonel, 73–74, 82, 147, 148, 153
Tsukahara, Fushizo, 56
Tulagi, 109
Tutuila, 8
Twenty-first Division (U.S.), 78
Twenty-sixty Cavalry (U.S.), 66, 78

U.S. Asiatic Fleet, 8, 9, 24, 62, 64, 68, 125–130
U.S. Pacific Fleet, 24, 158, 171
United States War Department, 142, 143
USS *Condor*, 33
USS *President Harrison*, 24
USS *Seal*, 63
Utah, 34–35

Van Ghent, 106
Van Nes, 106
Vestal, 34
Vincennes, 179, 181
Virginia, 34
Vizagapatam, 174

Wainwright, Jonathan M., 78, 139, 141, 144, 184; Japanese proclamation to, 140–141
Wake, 13, 40
Wake Island, 163–164, 168
Waller, Captain, 124
War Plan Orange No. 3, 65
Ward, 33
Wavell, Archibald, 73, 86, 89, 90, 92, 105, 111, 112, 114
West Virginia, 34
Whipple, 101, 125, 127
Wilderbeest bombers, 86
Wilkes, Captain, 77
William B. Preston, 108–109
Witte de With, 121
Wohlfield, Mark, 144

X-Day, 43

Y-Day, 29
Yamamoto, Isoroku, 18, 19,
    26–27, 28–31, 32, 35, 36,
    37, 38, 44, 134, 158, 160,
    166, 170, 171, 173, 174,
    175
Yamamoto plan, 18–19
Yamashita, Tomoyuki, 42–
    43, 46, 48, 49, 73–74, 75,
    84, 85, 86–89, 90–91

Yanagawa, Heisuke, 6
Yarnell, Henry, 8
Yorktown, 165, 169
Yura, 105

Zero fighters, 55, 86, 100,
    109
Zhukov, Marshal, 11
Zuikaku, 172